SANJEEV KAPOOR'S
Dakshin Delights

In association with Alyona Kapoor

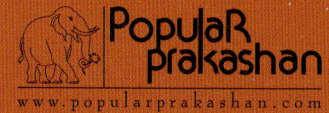
www.popularprakashan.com

Published by
POPULAR PRAKASHAN PVT. LTD.
301, Mahalaxmi Chambers
22, Bhulabhai Desai Road
Mumbai – 400 026
for KHANA KHAZANA PUBLICATIONS PVT. LTD.

© 2009 Sanjeev Kapoor

First Published 2009

WORLD RIGHTS RESERVED. The contents - all recipes, photographs and drawings are original and copyrighted. No portion of this book shall be reproduced, stored in a retrieval system or transmitted by any means, electronic, mechanical, photocopying, recording or otherwise, without the written permission of the author and the publisher.

(4148)
ISBN: 978-81-7991-400-7

Design: Mahendra Ghanekar & Anjali Sawant
Typesetting: Satyavan Rane

Printed in India
by Ajanta Offset & Packagings Ltd.
New Delhi-110 002

AUTHOR'S NOTE

Writing this book on South Indian food has been an enlightening experience. For the uninitiated, South Indian cuisine could mean food containing loads of curry leaves and coconut. The coastal states of the southern peninsula are verdant with coconut trees and the sea awash with plump seafood. The hills of the Deccan hinterland are covered with acres of spice groves that infuse the air with a fragrance that is not to be found anywhere else in the country.

There is so much to unearth and learn about the food of the south which differs from other cuisines of the country. There are numerous variations of rice dishes that can take a lifetime to discover, as well as varieties of *sambhar* and *rasam* that differ from household to household. It might take a population census to find out if the *sambhar* in one house has any resemblance to that of the neighbour's!

As you start turning the pages of this book, do not be overwhelmed by the complex names. The final dish that will be served is simplicity itself and so very easy to cook. You will also perfect the art of making batters of varying thickness and the use of the special coconut grater which produces delicate curls of coconut used to garnish dishes.

South Indian food comprises the foods from the four states of Andhra Pradesh, Karnataka, Kerala and Tamil Nadu. These cuisines are bound by a common thread – the predominant use of rice, *dal* and spices, dried red chillies, coconut and tamarind. The difference lies in the combination of spice and chillies, that determine the pungency and flavour of the food.

I consider the food from Andhra Pradesh to be the spiciest, as the special Guntur chillies are used lavishly with oil and slightly tempered with tamarind. Hyderabadi food is a part and parcel of this state's cuisine but I have written an entirely separate book on it. The mildest food could be from Karnataka where jaggery is used to counter the spices. Udupi food forms an integral part of this cuisine and our familiar *dosa* and *idli* and Mysore Paak are contributions from this state. Moving on to God's own country, Kerala, the food is a vast canvas with vegetarian fare for the Namboodiris and Nairs, while the Christian and Muslim communities favour non-vegetarian cuisine. Coconut plays an essential role in all food, and seafood is part of the daily diet along the coastal areas.

A typical Tamil meal, served on a banana leaf, sometimes has more than twenty items on one leaf! The star is the steamed rice, and when one is done with the *kozhambu* and *sambhar* course, side dishes like *kootu* and *poriyal* follow. The third course would be a variety of *vadai* and *bhajji*, chutneys and *pachadi*. The meal ends on a sweet note, *payasam* being an eternal favourite. What I must mention is Chettinad cuisine that is well known for its use of spices in non-vegetarian dishes. Chettiars love hot, pungent food and make the most of freshly ground *masala*.

As you explore the food that is enveloped in the aroma of cardamoms and peppercorns, rich with soothing coconut, remember all recipes in this book are meant to serve four people keeping in mind there are other complementary dishes in the meal. Let us cook together some Appam or Andhra Chilli Chicken or Puliyodharai or Set Dosa or Sakkarai Pongal. On second thoughts, I should replace the 'or' with 'and', and present you with a feast doused in southern spice.

Happy Cooking!

CONTENTS

Snacks and Starters 07

Vegetarian Main Course 25

Non-Vegetarian Main Course 45

Rice and Bread 63

Accompaniments 81

Sweets 93

SNACKS AND STARTERS

Kanchipuram Idli 08

Baby Uttapam 10

Meen Molaga Bhajji 11

Chicken 65 12

Kozhi Kara Vadai 14

Vazhakkai Chops 15

Chettinad Kozhi Varuval 16

Maddur Vade 18

Masala Dosa 19

Konju Porichatthu 20

Era Varuval 22

Set Dosa 23

KANCHIPURAM IDLI

Mildly spiced rice cakes steamed in banana leaves

Ingredients

1 cup rice

½ cup skinless split black gram

¾ teaspoon fenugreek seeds

1 teaspoon turmeric powder

20-25 black peppercorns

2 teaspoons split Bengal gram

A pinch of asafoetida

1 cup yogurt

½ cup pure ghee

Salt to taste

A few tender banana leaves

Method

1. Soak the rice and split black gram with the fenugreek seeds for three to four hours. Drain and grind to a smooth paste with sufficient water to make a thick batter.

2. Add the turmeric powder, peppercorns, split Bengal gram, asafoetida, yogurt, ghee and salt. Mix well and leave to ferment overnight, or for at least six hours.

3. Whip the batter and adjust the consistency. The batter should be fairly thick.

4. Heat sufficient water in a steamer. Line the *idli* moulds with the banana leaves and pour the batter into them. Place in the steamer and steam for about twenty minutes or till done.

5. Serve with Coconut Chutney (page 103) and Sambhar (page 90).

> Kanchipuram is as famous for its gorgeous silk sarees, as for the spicy idli which bears its name. Kanchipuram Idli are ideal for a wholesome breakfast.

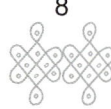

Tamil Nadu

BABY UTTAPAM

Small thick rice pancakes

Ingredients

1 cup rice
½ cup skinless split black gram
Salt to taste
Oil, as required

Topping

2 small onions, chopped
2 small tomatoes, seeded and chopped
2 green chillies, chopped

Method

1. Soak the rice in three cups of water, and the split black gram in two cups of water overnight, or for at least 6 hours. Drain and grind them separately to a smooth paste using a little water. Mix together both the batters in a deep pan or bowl. Cover and leave the batter to ferment for a minimum of six to eight hours in a warm place.

2. Add the salt and sufficient water to the batter to get the desired consistency and mix well.

3. Heat a heavy *tawa* or a non-stick pan. Add two drops of oil and wipe the *tawa* clean with a wet piece of muslin.

4. Add a tablespoon of oil to the *tawa* and heat it. Pour half a ladleful of batter and spread it into a three-inch round with the back of the ladle. Add more batter and make as many rounds as will fit on the *tawa*.

5. Sprinkle each *uttapam* with the onions, tomatoes and green chillies and cook over low heat for three to five minutes. Flip the *uttapam* over, if desired, and cook for a while longer. Serve hot.

| *Uttapam, also called Uttapa, is a popular breakfast dish in South India. All you need is fermented dosa batter and some vegetables. Small uttapam add variety and excitement to a morning meal.* |

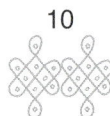

Tamil Nadu

MEEN MOLAGA BHAJJI

Deep-fried fish and capsicum fritters

Ingredients

1 Indian salmon fillet (300 grams)
2 medium green capsicums, cut into ½-inch wide strips
1 tablespoon lemon juice
1 teaspoon ginger paste
1 teaspoon garlic paste
1 tablespoon red chilli powder
Salt to taste
1 tablespoon rice flour
1 tablespoon refined flour
½ cup gram flour
¼ teaspoon soda bicarbonate
Oil for deep-frying

Method

1. Trim and cut the fish fillet into two-and-a-half inch by half-inch by half-inch fingers.

2. Mix together the lemon juice, ginger paste, garlic paste, chilli powder and salt to make a thick paste. Spread the paste uniformly over the fish fingers and the capsicum strips.

3. Mix together the rice flour, refined flour, gram flour and soda bicarbonate. Add sufficient water to make a smooth batter.

4. Sandwich each fish finger between two strips of capsicum. Secure well with toothpicks at both ends.

5. Heat sufficient oil in a *kadai*. Dip the prepared fish in the batter, shaking off the excess batter, and slide into the hot oil.

6. Fry over medium heat, turning over a couple of times, till crisp, golden brown and completely cooked. Drain on absorbent paper and serve with tomato sauce.

Tamil Nadu

CHICKEN 65

Hot and spicy chicken

Ingredients

450 grams boneless chicken, cut into 1½-inch pieces
½ cup yogurt
1½ tablespoons lemon juice
2 tablespoons rice flour
Salt to taste
6 tablespoons oil

Masala
4 dried red chillies
2 inches ginger
6 garlic cloves
2 tablespoons coriander seeds
12-15 black peppercorns

There are many stories of how this dish from Andhra Pradesh got its name. One is that guests would identify a dish by its number on the hotel menu. Maybe this popular chicken was the 65th item!

Method

1. Grind the ingredients for the *masala* to a fine paste.

2. Mix together the yogurt, lemon juice, rice flour, salt and two tablespoons oil into the ground *masala* paste.

3. Coat the chicken with the paste and marinate for an hour in a refrigerator.

4. Heat the remaining oil in a thick-bottomed *kadai*; add the chicken in small batches of six to eight pieces, and stir-fry over high heat for one minute, tossing continuously. Add another batch of the chicken and repeat.

5. Lower the heat once all the chicken has been added. Turn the pieces frequently, basting with the remaining *masala*.

6. Cook till the oil separates and the chicken turns crispy on the outside, but moist and soft on the inside.

7. Adjust salt, toss well and remove. Drain and serve hot.

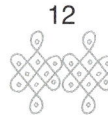

Andhra Pradesh

KOZHI KARA VADAI

Chicken fritters

Ingredients

250 grams boneless chicken
1 large potato, boiled and mashed
1 medium onion, chopped
2 tablespoons chopped fresh coriander
10-12 curry leaves, chopped
2 teaspoons ginger paste
2 teaspoons garlic paste
Salt to taste
Oil for deep-frying

Masala

¼ cup grated coconut
2 green chillies
4 dried red chillies
6 black peppercorns
2 inches cinnamon
2 cloves
¼ teaspoon cumin seeds
¼ teaspoon fennel seeds
¼ teaspoon poppy seeds

Method

1. Clean the chicken and mince well. Dry-roast all the ingredients for the *masala*, one by one, on a *tawa* and cool. Pound to a coarse powder.

2. Mix together the minced chicken, potato, onion, chopped coriander, curry leaves, ginger paste, garlic paste and the *masala* powder. Add salt to taste. Set aside for about half an hour to marinate.

3. Heat sufficient oil in a deep *kadai*.

4. Divide the chicken mixture into twenty-four equal balls. Flatten the balls between moistened palms and slide them, a few at a time, into the hot oil.

5. Deep-fry over medium heat till the *vadai* turn golden brown and are completely cooked. Drain on absorbent paper. Serve hot with any chutney.

Chef's Tip
Bite-sized *vadai* make the perfect cocktail snack.

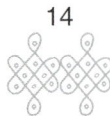

Tamil Nadu

VAZHAKKAI CHOPS
Spicy fried banana slices

Ingredients
4 (350 grams) unripe bananas

Salt to taste

½ teaspoon turmeric powder

20 curry leaves, chopped

1 teaspoon red chilli powder

1 teaspoon coriander powder

2 tablespoons rice flour

2 teaspoons Tamarind Pulp (page 103)

2 tablespoons oil + for shallow-frying

Method
1. Peel and slice the bananas lengthways into three to four slices. Cut each slice in half if too long.

2. Boil the banana slices in salted water to which the turmeric powder has been added, for five minutes. Drain and cool.

3. Mix together the curry leaves, chilli powder, coriander powder, rice flour, tamarind pulp and two tablespoons of oil. Spread the paste evenly over the banana slices. Set aside for fifteen minutes.

4. Heat sufficient oil in a pan and shallow-fry the banana slices till crisp and golden on both sides.

5. Drain on absorbent paper and serve hot.

Chef's Tip
Replace the bananas with sliced potatoes or yam.

Unripe bananas are a little sticky to peel and chop, so lightly oil the knife or peeler.

Tamil Nadu

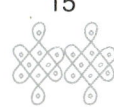

CHETTINAD KOZHI VARUVAL

Chettinad fried chicken

Ingredients

1 whole (800 grams) chicken
2 medium onions, roughly chopped
1 inch ginger, roughly chopped
4-6 garlic cloves, roughly chopped
4 green chillies, roughly chopped
4-6 dried red chillies
½ teaspoon turmeric powder
1 tablespoon lemon juice
2 tablespoons rice flour
Salt to taste
10-12 curry leaves, finely shredded
Oil for shallow-frying

| *Pungent with the flavour of curry leaves, this fried chicken needs plenty of time to marinate so do not make it if you are in a hurry.* |

Method

1. Split the chicken through the backbone and the breast, into two equal halves. Make three or four half-inch deep cuts on the breast and leg pieces.

2. Grind the onions, ginger, garlic, green chillies and red chillies with a little water to a smooth paste.

3. Mix the turmeric powder, lemon juice, rice flour and salt into the *masala* paste.

4. Coat the chicken liberally with the paste and leave to marinate for two or three hours, preferably in a refrigerator. Mix the shredded curry leaves into the chicken.

5. Heat the oil in a *kadai*; add the marinated chicken and sauté over high heat for two minutes on both sides to seal the juices.

6. Lower heat to medium, cover with a lid and cook for fifteen to twenty minutes, turning over and basting frequently with the remaining marinade. Sprinkle a little water if the chicken starts drying out.

7. Cook over high heat for the last few minutes, so that the surface of the chicken is crisp and golden brown.

8. Cut into smaller pieces and serve hot.

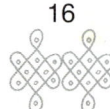

| *Tamil Nadu*

MADDUR VADE
Semolina and rice fritters

Ingredients
½ cup semolina
½ cup rice flour
½ cup refined flour
5 green chillies, chopped
2 onions, chopped
2 tablespoons chopped fresh coriander
3 tablespoons melted ghee
Salt to taste
Oil for deep-frying

Maddur Vade is probably named after Maddur, a small town in Mandya district of Karnataka, halfway between Bangalore and Mysore, where travellers stop for the popular snack.

Method

1. Mix together all the ingredients except oil, adding a very little water, and make a stiff dough.

2. To make each *vada*, place a ladleful of dough on the palm of one hand and flatten it with the other hand.

3. Heat sufficient oil in a *kadai* and deep-fry the *vade*, a few at a time, until golden brown and crisp.

4. Drain on absorbent paper. Serve hot or cold with any chutney.

Karnataka

MASALA DOSA

Rice pancakes with a potato stuffing

Ingredients

2¾ cups parboiled rice
¼ cup raw rice
1 cup skinless split black gram
1 teaspoon fenugreek seeds
Salt to taste
Oil, as required

Potato Stuffing

3 large potatoes, boiled, peeled and cubed
1 tablespoon oil
½ teaspoon mustard seeds
¼ teaspoon asafoetida
1 teaspoon split Bengal gram
2 green chillies, chopped
6-8 curry leaves
1 large onion, chopped
½ teaspoon turmeric powder
Salt to taste
2 tablespoons chopped fresh coriander leaves
1 tablespoon lemon juice

Method

1. Wash both the varieties of rice two or three times and soak in six cups of water for at least four hours. Wash and soak the split black gram with fenugreek seeds in three cups of water for a similar length of time.

2. Drain and grind the rice and split black gram separately to make smooth batters of dropping consistency. Mix together both the batters thoroughly, with your hand in a whipping motion. Add salt.

3. Pour the batter into a large vessel, cover tightly and leave to ferment overnight or for at least four to six hours at room temperature.

4. To make the potato stuffing, heat the oil in a *kadai*. Add the mustard seeds and when they begin to splutter, add the asafoetida and split Bengal gram and sauté till lightly browned. Add the green chillies, curry leaves and onion and sauté till the onion is lightly browned.

5. Add the potatoes, turmeric powder and salt and mix well. Sprinkle a tablespoon of water and cook till the potatoes are heated through. Add the chopped coriander and lemon juice and mix well.

6. Mix the batter well, adjusting it to pouring consistency. Heat a flat *tawa* (preferably non-stick), and grease it with a little oil. Pour a ladleful of batter and spread to as thin a pancake as possible with the back of the ladle. A couple of *dosa* may go wrong, but once the *tawa* is seasoned, the rest of the *dosa* will come out well.

7. Pour the oil around the *dosa* and let it cook till the edges become crisp and golden brown. Place about four tablespoons of potato stuffing in the centre of the *dosa*, fold to the desired shape and serve hot.

Karnataka

KONJU PORICHATTHU

Spicy fried prawns

Ingredients

32 (300 grams) medium prawns, peeled and deveined
1½ teaspoons lemon juice
Salt to taste
15 curry leaves
4 green chillies
15 garlic cloves
½ teaspoon carom seeds
1 tablespoon red chilli powder
¼ cup rice flour
¼ teaspoon soda bicarbonate
Oil for deep-frying

| *A memorable combination of crisp prawns and spicy curry leaves.* |

Method

1. Wash and drain the prawns. Pat them dry with a clean kitchen towel.

2. Marinate the prawns in a mixture of lemon juice and salt.

3. Grind the curry leaves, green chillies and garlic with half a teaspoon of lemon juice to a smooth paste. Crush the carom seeds lightly and mix into the paste along with the chilli powder.

4. Coat the prawns with the spice paste and marinate for fifteen to twenty minutes, preferably in a refrigerator.

5. Add the rice flour and mix well.

6. Heat sufficient oil in a *kadai* and slide the prawns into the hot oil, a few at a time. Turn over and deep-fry till golden brown and crisp. Drain on absorbent paper.

7. Serve hot with any sauce or chutney.

Chef's Tip
Substitute prawns with fish, crabmeat, squid or mussels.

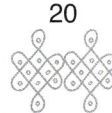

Kerala

ERA VARUVAL
Stir-fried prawns

Ingredients

16 (160 grams) medium prawns, peeled and deveined
1 inch ginger
6-8 garlic cloves
1 teaspoon cumin powder
1 tablespoon Tamarind Pulp (page 103)
2 tablespoons red chilli powder
½ teaspoon turmeric powder
Salt to taste
2 tablespoons rice flour
¼ cup oil
1 tablespoon lemon juice

Method

1. Pat the prawns dry with a clean kitchen towel. Grind the ginger and garlic to a fine paste.

2. Mix together the ginger-garlic paste, cumin powder, tamarind pulp, chilli powder, turmeric powder, salt, rice flour and two tablespoons of oil.

3. Marinate the prawns in the mixture for at least two hours, preferably in a refrigerator.

4. Heat the remaining oil in a pan; add the marinated prawns and cook for a minute over high heat. Turn the prawns over and cook for another minute. Lower the heat and cook for two to three minutes, turning the prawns occasionally to cook evenly.

5. Remove the prawns, drain on absorbent paper, sprinkle lemon juice and serve hot.

Tamil Nadu

SET DOSA
Thick rice pancakes

Ingredients
2 cups rice
½ teaspoon fenugreek seeds
1 cup beaten rice
1 cup yogurt
Salt to taste
Oil, as required

> The longer the batter is fermented, the spongier the dosa! The beaten rice helps to bind the batter and makes the dosa lighter.

Method

1. Wash and soak the rice and fenugreek seeds in four cups of warm water for about two hours.

2. Soak the beaten rice in a little water for about five minutes. Grind the rice and fenugreek seeds along with the beaten rice and salt into a smooth, thick batter. Add the yogurt and salt and mix well. Keep the batter in a warm place to ferment overnight.

3. Heat a *tawa* and grease it. For each *dosa*, pour a ladleful of batter onto the *tawa*, but do not spread it. The batter will set in a thick round. Drizzle a little oil all around the *dosa* and cover it with a lid. Cook till the underside is done and very light brown. Serve hot with Sambhar (page 90) or Coconut Chutney (page 103).

Chef's Tip
For added flavour, grind green chillies and ginger with the rest of the ingredients.

Karnataka

VEGETARIAN MAIN COURSE

Murungakkai Kozhambu 26
Aviyal 28
Kakkarkai Pullusu 29
Donne Mirsang Kayras 30
Chidambaram Ambat 32
Beans Poriyal 33
Mathanga Erisery 34
Ennai Kathrikai 36
Kaikari Ishtew 37
Poondu Kozhambu 38
Kalan 40
Rasakalan 41
Paruppu Urundai Kozhambu 42
Soppina Palya 43

MURUNGAKKAI KOZHAMBU
Drumstick curry

Ingredients

6 (220 grams) drumsticks, cut into 2-inch pieces
2 tablespoons oil
4 medium onions, sliced
4 green chillies, slit
1½ cups Thin Coconut Milk (page 103)
1½ tablespoons Tamarind Pulp (page 103)
1 teaspoon Madras curry powder
Salt to taste
1 cup Thick Coconut Milk (page 103)
7-8 curry leaves
2 tablespoons chopped fresh coriander

Method

1. Heat the oil in a pan; add the onions and sauté till translucent. Add the green chillies and stir for half a minute.

2. Add the drumsticks and thin coconut milk. Cover and cook over low heat till the drumsticks are tender.

3. Add the tamarind pulp, curry powder and salt to taste. Stir well and cook over low heat for four to five minutes. Add the thick coconut milk and bring to a boil.

4. Remove from heat and serve hot, garnished with the curry leaves and fresh coriander.

| *Drumsticks are fascinating as the inner flesh is sweet and the outer skin tough and hard. A versatile vegetable, it can be added to sambar and aviyal and is delicious cooked with shrimp.* |

Tamil Nadu

AVIYAL

Mixed vegetables in coconut and yogurt

Ingredients
1 medium carrot
6-8 French beans
6-8 broad beans
200 grams white pumpkin
1 medium unripe banana
1 drumstick
100 grams yam
¼ cup shelled green peas
Salt to taste
½ cup grated fresh coconut
4 green chillies
1½ teaspoons cumin seeds
1 tablespoon rice
1½ cups yogurt
10-12 curry leaves
2 tablespoons coconut oil

Method

1. Cut the carrot, French beans, broad beans, pumpkin, banana, drumstick and yam into thick fingers not more than two inches long.

2. Boil the yam in salted water, drain and reserve.

3. Grind the coconut, green chillies, cumin seeds and rice with a little water, to a fine paste. Whisk the yogurt with the ground paste and set aside.

4. Boil the rest of the vegetables in one and a half cups of water, adding salt and the curry leaves.

5. When the vegetables are almost done, add the yogurt mixture and yam and stir thoroughly. Bring to simmering point and remove from heat.

6. Stir in the coconut oil and serve hot.

Chef's Tips
- If you do not like the smell of raw coconut oil, heat the oil, add the curry leaves and add to the *aviyal*.
- You can also add unripe mango to *aviyal*; in which case, reduce the yogurt to only one cup. As far as possible, *aviyal* should never be reheated.

Kerala

KAKKARKAI PULLUSU

Curried bitter gourd

Ingredients

4-5 medium bitter gourds
Salt to taste
1 inch ginger
5 garlic cloves
4 dried red chillies
1 tablespoon coriander seeds
1 teaspoon cumin seeds
1 teaspoon white sesame seeds
1½ teaspoons oil
2 medium onions, chopped
¼ cup tomato purée
2 tablespoons grated jaggery
2 tablespoons Tamarind Pulp (page 103)

Method

1. Wash, scrape and cut the bitter gourds lengthways in half; remove the seeds and slice thinly. Rub with some salt and set aside for ten or fifteen minutes. Rinse in plenty of water, drain and squeeze out the excess water. This will remove some of the bitterness.

2. Grind the ginger and garlic to a fine paste.

3. Dry-roast the red chillies, coriander seeds, cumin seeds and sesame seeds on a medium hot *tawa* till light brown, stirring continuously. Cool the mixture and grind to a fine powder.

4. Heat the oil in a non-stick pan and add the bitter gourds and stir-fry for four to five minutes or slightly browned. Add chopped onions and stir-fry for three to four minutes.

5. Add the ginger-garlic paste and stir-fry for one or two minutes. Add the tomato purée and cook for a few minutes longer.

6. Add the ground spice powder, grated jaggery, tamarind pulp and salt. Stir well and add one cup of water and bring the mixture to a boil.

7. Lower the heat to medium, cover and simmer for five minutes. Serve with rice or *roti*.

Andhra Pradesh

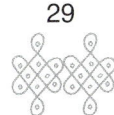

DONNE MIRSANG KAYRAS

Capsicums, potatoes and peanuts in a sweet and sour coconut gravy

Ingredients

5-6 medium green capsicums, cut into 1-inch pieces

2 medium potatoes, cut into 1-inch cubes

½ cup raw peanuts

1 tablespoon oil

½ teaspoon mustard seeds

A pinch of asafoetida

¼ teaspoon turmeric powder

Salt to taste

1½ tablespoons grated jaggery

Masala

½ cup grated coconut

3 tablespoons sesame seeds

½ tablespoon oil

2 tablespoons split Bengal gram

2 tablespoons coriander seeds

¼ teaspoon fenugreek seeds

4-5 dried red chillies (Bedgi)

2 tablespoons Tamarind Pulp (page 103)

Method

1. For the *masala*, separately dry-roast the coconut and sesame seeds in a pan till fragrant and lightly coloured. Transfer to a plate and set aside to cool.

2. Heat half a tablespoon of oil in the same pan; add the split Bengal gram, coriander seeds, fenugreek seeds and red chillies and sauté till fragrant. Grind along with the roasted coconut and sesame seeds, and the tamarind pulp to a fine paste with three-fourth cup of water.

3. Heat one tablespoon oil in a pan; add the mustard seeds and when they begin to splutter, add the asafoetida. Add the peanuts and sauté for three to four minutes.

4. Add the potatoes, turmeric powder, salt and jaggery. Stir, cover and cook over low heat for five minutes. Add the capsicums, stir and cook till the vegetables are partially cooked.

5. Add the ground paste and one and a half cups of water, and cook over low heat for three to four minutes. Serve hot.

A Saraswat Brahmin delicacy with an unusual sweet and sour taste, it is an essential dish on a wedding menu.

Karnataka

CHIDAMBARAM AMBAT
Tangy ridge gourd

Ingredients

450 grams ridge gourd, peeled and cut into 1-inch pieces

A small lemon-sized ball of tamarind

1 tablespoon oil

1 teaspoon mustard seeds

1½ medium onions, sliced

½ teaspoon red chilli powder

½ teaspoon turmeric powder

Salt to taste

½ teaspoon freshly ground black peppercorns

2 medium tomatoes, chopped

Method

1. Soak the tamarind in half a cup of warm water for five minutes. Strain the pulp and set aside.

2. Heat the oil in a pan and add the mustard seeds. When they begin to splutter, add the onions and sauté until lightly browned. Add the chilli powder, turmeric powder, salt and freshly ground peppercorns. Sauté for a minute and then add the tomatoes and ridge gourd.

3. Cover and cook over low heat for ten minutes, stirring occasionally.

4. Stir in the tamarind pulp and cook, uncovered until nearly dry. Serve hot.

| *Cooked in a flavourful masala, the simple ridge gourd takes on a new avatar!*

Tamil Nadu

BEANS PORIYAL

French beans with coconut

Ingredients
250 grams French beans, cut into ¼-inch pieces
2-3 tablespoons oil
½ teaspoon mustard seeds
1 teaspoon skinless split black gram
A pinch of asafoetida
2 dried red chillies, broken into bits
8-10 curry leaves
Salt to taste
¼ cup grated coconut

Method

1. Heat the oil in a pan. Add the mustard seeds and split black gram and sauté till the gram turns light brown.

2. Add the asafoetida and red chillies and sauté for half a minute.

3. Add the French beans, curry leaves and salt. Add half the coconut and mix well. Cover and cook over medium heat for five minutes. Garnish with the remaining coconut and serve hot.

> Some cooks boil the beans before preparing this dish. Either way, it makes an excellent accompaniment to rice with hot sambhar.

Chef's Tip
Use a special coconut grater to get the delicate coconut curls that enhance the appearance of the dish.

Tamil Nadu

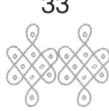

MATHANGA ERISERY

Pumpkin in a lentil and coconut gravy

Ingredients

250 grams red pumpkin, cut into ½-inch cubes

¼ cup split pigeon peas, soaked

2 tablespoons oil

½ teaspoon mustard seeds

2 dried red chillies, broken into two

10-12 curry leaves

1 small onion, chopped

Salt to taste

Masala

½ cup grated coconut

2 dried red chillies

½ teaspoon cumin seeds

3 garlic cloves

Salt to taste

Method

1. Drain and boil the split pigeon peas in one and three-fourth cup of water or pressure-cook till tender. Cool and mash with a wooden ladle till smooth.

2. Grind the ingredients for the *masala* to a coarse paste.

3. Heat the oil in a pan and add the mustard seeds. When they begin to splutter, add the red chillies, curry leaves and onion and sauté till lightly browned.

4. Add the pumpkin and stir. Cover and cook over medium heat till the pumpkin is tender but firm.

5. Add the pigeon peas, ground mixture and salt and mix well. Simmer for two to three minutes and serve hot.

A traditional Kerala dish, erisery is made with pumpkin, yam or unripe bananas.

Kerala

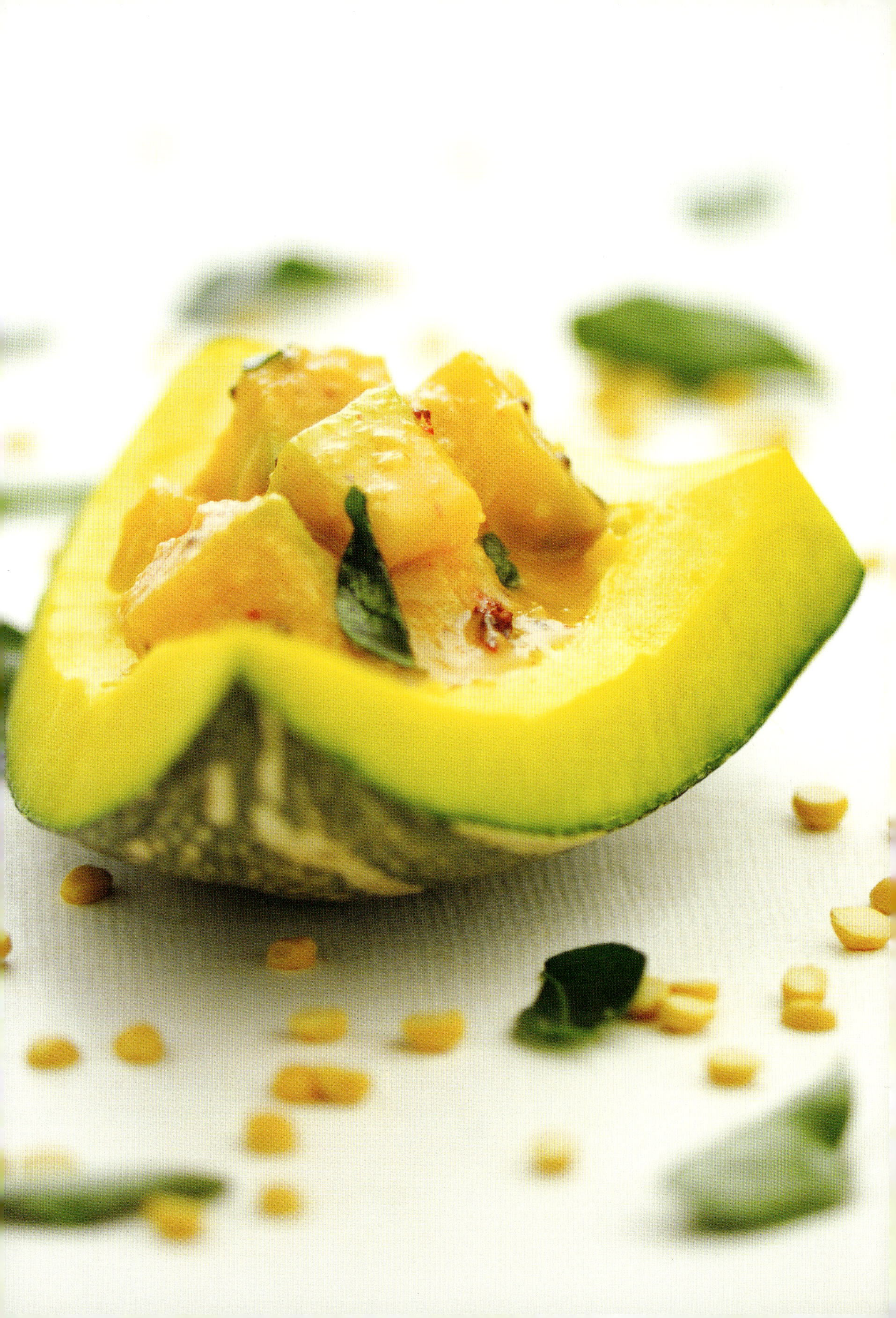

ENNAI KATHRIKAI

Spicy stuffed brinjals

Ingredients

16-20 baby brinjals

¼ cup oil

10 curry leaves

1 tablespoon Tamarind Pulp (page 103)

Masala

2 tablespoons oil

½ teaspoon mustard seeds

½ teaspoon cumin seeds

¼ teaspoon fenugreek seeds

2 tablespoons coriander seeds

1 tablespoon split Bengal gram

1 tablespoon skinless split black gram

4 dried red chillies

10 black peppercorns

¼ teaspoon asafoetida

¼ teaspoon turmeric powder

10-12 curry leaves, finely chopped

½ cup grated coconut

Salt to taste

Method

1. Trim the heads of the brinjals and slit into four without separating the segments.

2. For the *masala*, heat two tablespoons of oil and fry all the ingredients except the coconut. Remove from heat and mix in the coconut. Grind coarsely when completely cold and add salt.

3. Fill the slit brinjals with the *masala*.

4. Heat one-fourth cup of oil in a *kadai*; add the curry leaves and the stuffed brinjals. Spread the remaining *masala*, if any, on top of the brinjals, cover the pan and cook for a few minutes.

5. Mix the tamarind pulp with a little water and mix gently into the brinjals. Add another quarter cup of water if the dish is too dry. Cover and cook over medium heat for fifteen to twenty minutes. Serve hot.

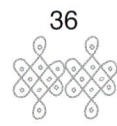

Tamil Nadu

KAIKARI ISHTEW

Mixed vegetables stewed in mildly-spiced coconut milk

Ingredients

2 medium carrots, cubed

2 medium potatoes, cubed

7-8 cauliflower florets

6–8 French beans, cut into 1-inch pieces

2 tablespoons coconut oil

2 bay leaves

2 one-inch cinnamon sticks

4 cloves

2 star anise

10–12 curry leaves

4 green chillies, slit

2 medium onions, chopped

2 teaspoons ginger-garlic paste

1 cup Thin Coconut Milk (page 103)

Salt to taste

1 cup Thick Coconut Milk (page 103)

A pinch of *garam masala* powder

Method

1. Parboil the carrots, potatoes, cauliflower florets and French beans separately. Drain and set aside.

2. Heat the coconut oil in a deep pan. Add the bay leaves, cinnamon, cloves, star anise, curry leaves, green chillies and onions, and sauté for two minutes.

3. Add the ginger-garlic paste, stir and cook for a minute.

4. Add the carrots, potatoes, cauliflower and the thin coconut milk and cook for two to three minutes. Add the salt and the French beans and cook till the French beans are tender.

5. Stir in the thick coconut milk and the *garam masala*. Remove from heat immediately and serve hot with Appam (page 78).

Appam and stew are the dal-roti of Kerala.

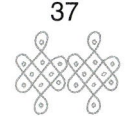

Kerala

POONDU KOZHAMBU
Garlic curry

Ingredients

1 cup (55-60) garlic cloves

2 tablespoons sesame oil

2 teaspoons split pigeon peas

10-12 dried red chillies, broken into bits

2 teaspoons coriander seeds

10-12 black peppercorns

1 teaspoon fenugreek seeds

4 teaspoons grated coconut

10-12 curry leaves

2 tablespoons Tamarind Pulp (page 103)

¼ teaspoon turmeric powder

Salt to taste

A pinch of asafoetida

1 teaspoon rice flour

Method

1. Heat the oil in a *kadai* and roast the split pigeon peas, red chillies, coriander seeds, peppercorns and fenugreek seeds till fragrant. Add the coconut, garlic and curry leaves and sauté for two to three minutes. Grind together to a smooth paste.

2. Bring one cup of water to a boil in a pan and add the tamarind pulp, turmeric powder, salt and asafoetida. Cook over low heat till the raw aroma of the tamarind disappears.

3. Add the ground paste and simmer till the curry thickens.

4. Mix the rice flour in two tablespoons of water and add to the curry. Cook for another three to four minutes, stirring continuously. Serve hot or cold.

This dish is an example of how garlic should be treated: with reverence! This curry is superb with hot steamed rice.

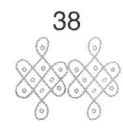

Tamil Nadu

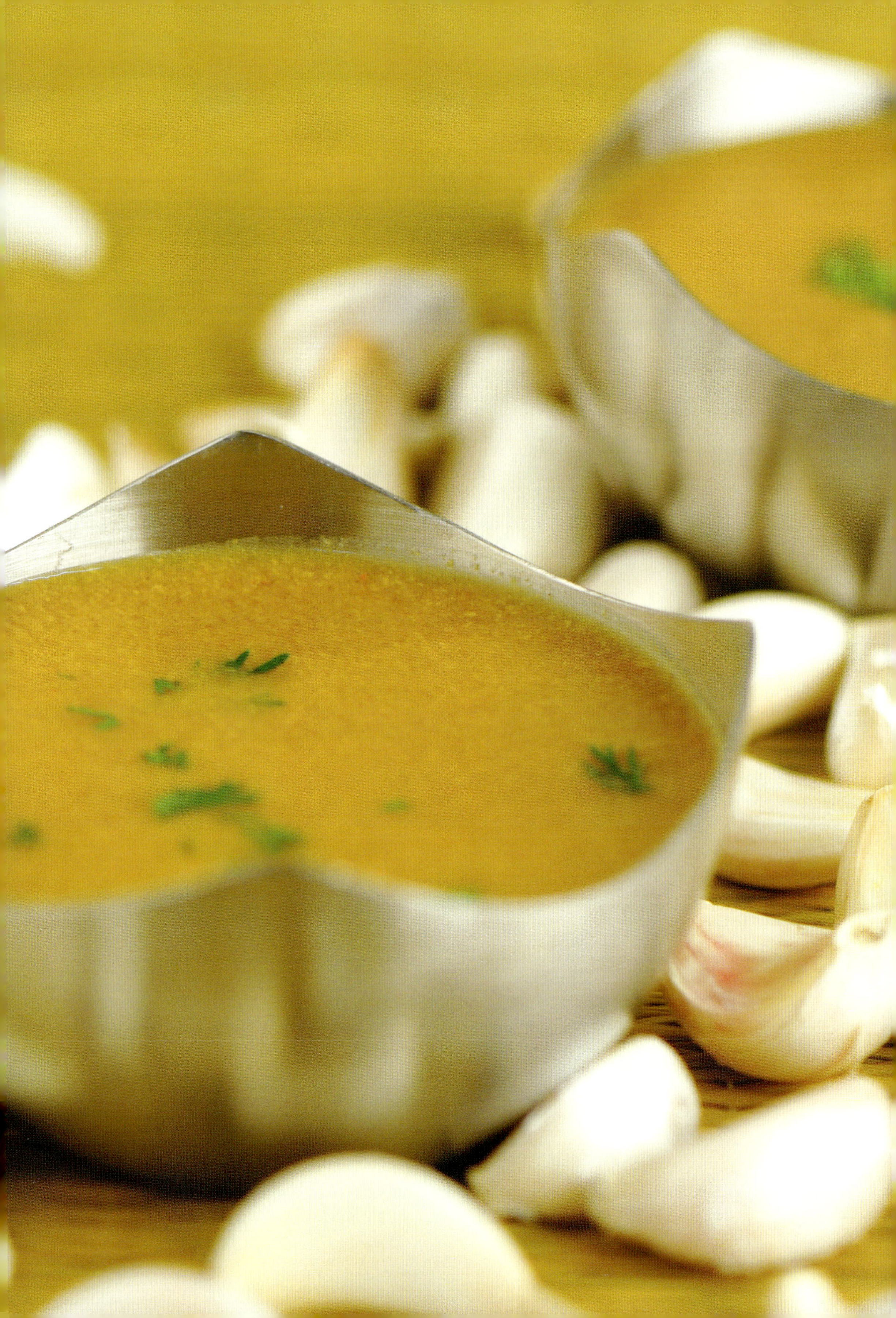

KALAN

Mixed vegetables in a yogurt and coconut curry

Ingredients

300 grams yam
2 unripe bananas
200 grams bottle gourd
1 cup grated coconut
4 green chillies
Salt to taste
½ teaspoon turmeric powder
2 cups yogurt, whisked
10-12 curry leaves
2 tablespoons coconut oil
1 teaspoon mustard seeds
2 dried red chillies, broken into bits

A favourite of Malayalis, kalan forms an important part of a sitdown festive sadya served in traditional style on a banana leaf.

Method

1. Peel and cut the yam, bananas and bottle gourd into medium-sized fingers.

2. Grind the coconut and green chillies to a smooth paste.

3. Bring one cup of water to a boil in a deep pan with a little salt and turmeric powder. Add the vegetables and simmer till half cooked. Stir in the whisked yogurt, bring to a boil and cook over low heat.

4. With a flat perforated spoon keep skimming the creamy layer from the top and reserve in a bowl. Continue doing this till only the whey is left in the curry.

5. Add the curry leaves and salt to taste and cook till the liquid reduces by half.

6. Mix the coconut-chilli paste with the reserved skimmed cream and add to the vegetables. Cook for a couple of minutes and remove from heat.

7. Heat the coconut oil in a pan and add the mustard seeds. When they begin to splutter add the red chillies and pour over the curry. Cover immediately to trap the aroma of the spices. Serve hot.

Chef's Tip
Use thin buttermilk instead of water to cook the vegetables for a better flavour and aroma.

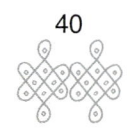

Kerala

RASAKALAN

Ash gourd in a yogurt gravy

Ingredients

200 grams ash gourd, cut into ½-inch cubes

2 cups yogurt, whisked

4 teaspoons coconut oil

1 teaspoon fenugreek seeds

2-3 dried red chillies

1 cup grated coconut

2-3 green chillies

1 teaspoon raw rice

2 tablespoons grated jaggery

Salt to taste

½ teaspoon turmeric powder

1 teaspoon mustard seeds

1 dried red chilli, halved

10-12 curry leaves

Rasa means 'very tasty' in Malayalam and Tamil. Need we say more!

Method

1. Heat two teaspoons of oil in a pan. Add the fenugreek seeds and red chillies and sauté till fragrant. Grind together with the coconut, green chillies and rice to a smooth paste with two to three tablespoons of water.

2. Add the paste to the yogurt along with the jaggery and salt and whisk till well blended.

3. Bring one cup of water to a boil in a deep pan; add the ash gourd and turmeric powder. Lower the heat and cook for five minutes or until the ash gourd is tender. Drain and set aside.

4. For the seasoning, heat the remaining oil in a deep pan; add the mustard seeds and when they begin to splutter, add the red chilli and curry leaves.

5. Add the yogurt mixture and the boiled ash gourd and cook over low heat, stirring continuously to prevent curdling, till the gravy just comes to a boil. Remove from heat immediately and serve hot with rice.

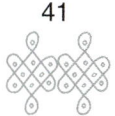

Kerala

PARUPPU URUNDAI KOZHAMBU

Lentil dumplings in a tamarind-flavoured curry

Ingredients

1 cup split pigeon peas
¼ cup split Bengal gram
8 dried red chillies
5 tablespoons oil
A pinch of asafoetida
1 teaspoon mustard seeds
1 medium onion, chopped
2 green chillies, chopped
¼ cup grated coconut
Salt to taste
20 curry leaves
¼ cup chopped fresh coriander
1 tablespoon rice flour
½ teaspoon fenugreek seeds
1½ teaspoons Sambhar Powder (page 103)
1½ tablespoons Tamarind Pulp (page 103)

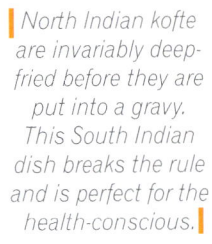

| *North Indian kofte are invariably deep-fried before they are put into a gravy. This South Indian dish breaks the rule and is perfect for the health-conscious.* |

Method

1. Soak the split pigeon peas and split Bengal gram in four cups of water for half an hour. Drain completely and crush with six red chillies.

2. Heat half the oil in a pan. Add the asafoetida, half the mustard seeds, the onion and green chillies and sauté for a few minutes. Add the coconut and the crushed mixture and sauté for a while longer. Stir in the salt and cook for five to eight minutes. Remove from heat and set aside to cool for a while.

3. Chop half the curry leaves and add to the coconut mixture along with half the fresh coriander and the rice flour. Mix well to make a dough. Shape into small balls (*kofte*).

4. Heat the remaining oil in a pan. Break the remaining red chillies into pieces and add along with the remaining mustard seeds, the fenugreek seeds, the remaining curry leaves, *sambhar* powder and one and a half cups of water. Mix well. When the mixture comes to a boil, add salt and slide in the *kofte*.

5. Stir in the tamarind pulp and remaining fresh coriander. Cover and cook over medium heat for about ten minutes till the gravy is thick and the *kofte* are cooked. Serve hot.

Tamil Nadu

SOPPINA PALYA

Steamed amaranth leaves with peanuts

Ingredients

4 bunches (175 grams each) amaranth leaves, chopped

1 tablespoon oil

1 teaspoon mustard seeds

8-10 garlic cloves

4 dried red chillies, broken into bits

15-20 curry leaves

Salt to taste

2 tablespoons roasted peanuts, coarsely powdered

> The same recipe can be made with other greens like spinach or fenugreek. Served with hot jolada rotti (jowar roti) in Karnataka it makes for a good wholesome meal.

Method

1. Heat the oil in a pan; add the mustard seeds, garlic cloves, red chillies and curry leaves and sauté till fragrant.

2. Add the amaranth leaves and stir. Cover and cook over medium heat till almost tender.

3. Add the salt and cook till all the water evaporates. Set aside to cool slightly.

4. Garnish with the peanut powder and serve.

Karnataka

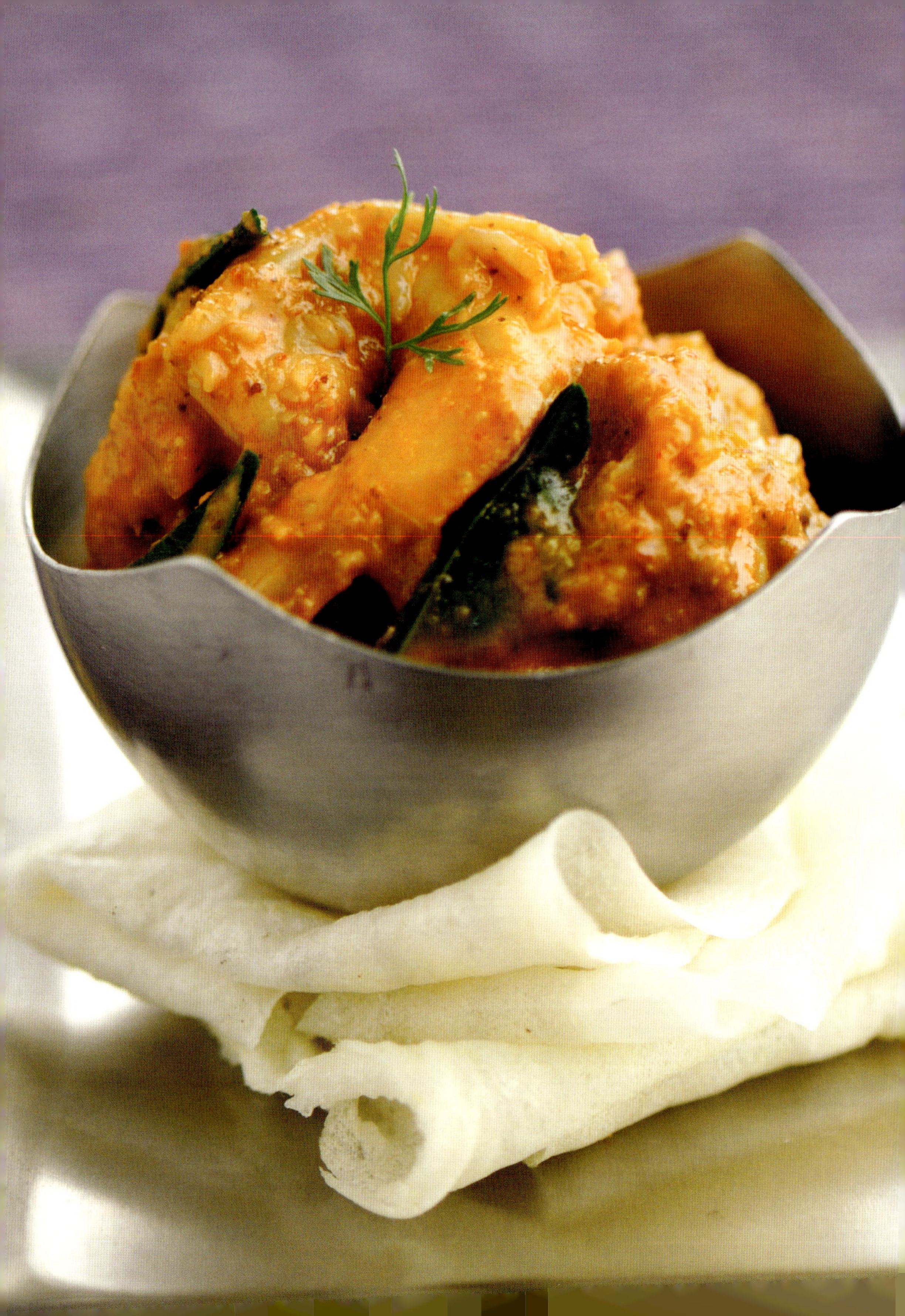

NON-VEGETARIAN MAIN COURSE

Mutton Urundai Kozhambu 46

Kori Ghassi 48

Maamsam Koora 49

Inji Kari Kozhambu 50

Iggaru Royya 52

Andhra Chilli Chicken 53

Nandu Milagu Kozhambu 54

Chettinad Kozhi Milagu Varuval 56

Fish Moilee 57

Eratchi Olathiyathu 58

Kozhi Thengai Kozhambu 60

MUTTON URUNDAI KOZHAMBU

Meatball curry

Ingredients

450 grams minced mutton
2 tablespoons mutton fat
2 eggs
1 lemon-sized ball of tamarind
¼ cup chopped fresh coriander
1 teaspoon turmeric powder
Salt to taste
8 tablespoons oil
2 medium onions, chopped
2 medium tomatoes, puréed

Masala Paste

1 inch ginger, roughly chopped
4-5 garlic cloves, roughly chopped
4 green chillies, roughly chopped
2 teaspoons poppy seeds, soaked in warm water
¼ cup grated coconut

Masala Powder

2 dried red chillies
15 black peppercorns
2 tablespoons split Bengal gram
2 tablespoons coriander seeds
1 inch cinnamon
2 cloves
1 star anise
2 green cardamoms
¼ teaspoon grated nutmeg

Method

1. Wash the minced mutton and pound the mutton fat into it till well blended. Mix in the eggs lightly.

2. Soak the tamarind in two cups of warm water; extract the pulp and strain. For the *masala* paste, grind together the ginger, garlic, green chillies, poppy seeds and coconut to a fine paste.

3. Dry-roast the ingredients for the *masala* powder, cool and grind to a coarse powder.

4. Mix half the fresh coriander, the turmeric powder, salt and one-fourth of the *masala* paste and one-fourth of the *masala* powder into the minced mutton and set aside for at least an hour to marinate, preferably in a refrigerator.

5. Divide the mince mixture into sixteen equal portions, moisten your palms and shape the mixture into smooth balls. Cover with a damp cloth and set aside.

6. Heat the oil in a wide, shallow pan; add the onions and sauté till golden brown. Add the remaining *masala* paste and continue to cook for a while.

7. Pour in the puréed tomatoes, tamarind pulp and one cup of water. Cook over medium heat for five to six minutes, or till the oil separates. Add the remaining *masala* powder, stir and simmer for a minute, adding a little more water if required.

8. Gently slide the mutton balls into the gravy and cook over low heat for fifteen minutes, or till the mutton balls are cooked. Serve hot, garnished with the remaining fresh coriander.

Tamil Nadu

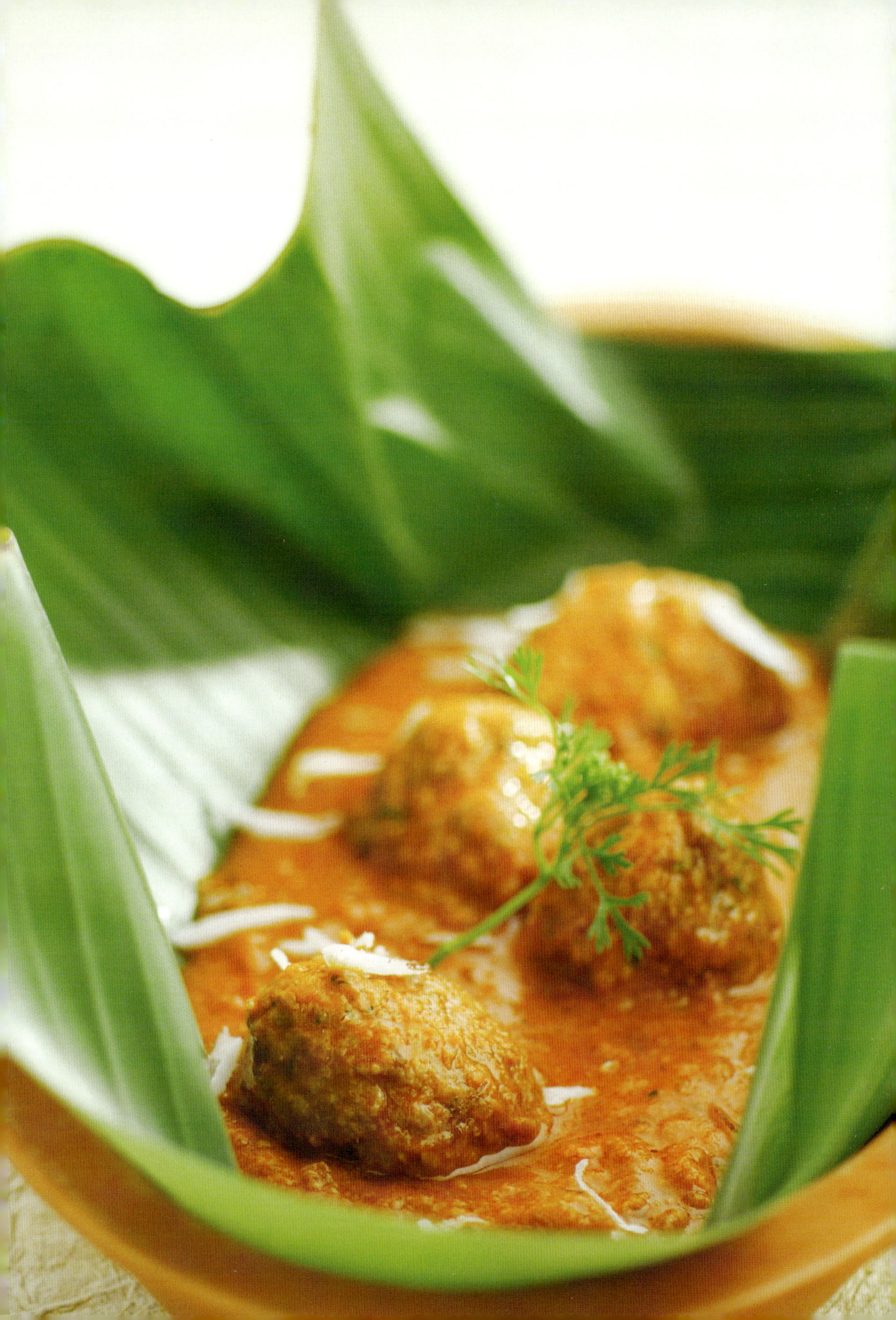

KORI GHASSI

Chicken curry

Ingredients

1 whole chicken (800 grams), cut into 1-inch pieces

2 tablespoons coriander seeds

1 teaspoon cumin seeds

1 teaspoon mustard seeds

10 dried red chillies

8 black peppercorns

1 cup grated coconut

10 garlic cloves

2 medium onions, sliced

2 tablespoons coconut oil

10-12 curry leaves

2 medium tomatoes, chopped

Salt to taste

1 cup Thick Coconut Milk (page 103)

2 tablespoons chopped fresh coriander

A popular Mangalorean chicken curry, this coconut-flavoured ghassi is excellent with rice.

Method

1. Dry-roast the coriander seeds, cumin seeds, mustard seeds, red chillies, peppercorns and coconut one by one and set aside to cool. Add the garlic and one-fourth of the sliced onions to the roasted ingredients and grind to a fine paste.

2. Heat the coconut oil in a deep pan. Add the remaining onions and curry leaves and sauté till golden brown. Add the tomatoes and salt and sauté for two to three minutes, or till the tomatoes turn pulpy.

3. Add the chicken and sauté for two to three minutes. Add the ground paste and mix well. Cover and cook over medium heat till the chicken is tender.

4. Stir in the coconut milk and adjust seasoning. Simmer for two to three minutes.

5. Garnish with the fresh coriander and serve hot.

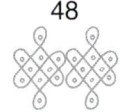

Karnataka

MAAMSAM KOORA
Mutton curry

Ingredients

500 grams boneless mutton, cubed

Salt to taste

¼ teaspoon turmeric powder

1 teaspoon poppy seeds

½ teaspoon fennel seeds

4 black peppercorns

1 teaspoon coriander seeds

1 teaspoon cumin seeds

1 inch cinnamon

2 cloves

2 green cardamoms

4 tablespoons oil

10 curry leaves

3 medium onions, chopped

1 teaspoon ginger-garlic paste

½ teaspoon red chilli powder

2 teaspoons black pepper powder

1 large tomato, chopped

2 tablespoons chopped fresh coriander

Method

1. Pressure cook the mutton with two cups of water, salt and turmeric powder till the pressure is released six times (six whistles). Remove the lid when the pressure reduces, drain and reserve the cooking liquid.

2. Dry-roast the poppy seeds, fennel seeds, peppercorns, coriander seeds, cumin seeds, cinnamon, cloves and cardamoms. Cool and grind to a fine powder.

3. Heat the oil in *kadai*. Add the curry leaves and onions and sauté till the onions are browned.

4. Add the ginger-garlic paste, chilli powder and half the pepper powder and sauté for a minute.

5. Add the tomato and mutton and cook on high heat till the tomato softens.

6. Add the salt and spice powder and cook on low heat for five minutes. Add the reserved cooking liquid and one cup of water and bring to a boil. Lower the heat and simmer till the gravy thickens and coats the mutton.

7. Add the remaining pepper powder and stir well. Garnish with the chopped coriander and serve hot.

Andhra Pradesh

INJI KARI KOZHAMBU

Mutton in a ginger-flavoured curry

Ingredients

500 grams boneless mutton, cut into 1-inch pieces
3 teaspoons ginger paste
1 teaspoon red chilli powder
1 teaspoon coriander powder
½ teaspoon turmeric powder
Salt to taste
1 cup grated coconut
2 tablespoons oil
1 inch cinnamon
2 cloves
2 green cardamoms
2 medium onions, chopped
6 green chillies, slit
1 teaspoon ginger-garlic paste
½ cup chopped fresh coriander leaves

Method

1. Mix together the ginger paste, chilli powder, coriander powder, turmeric powder and salt in a bowl. Add the mutton and mix well. Set aside to marinate for one hour, preferably in a refrigerator.

2. Grind the coconut with one cup of warm water. Strain to extract thick coconut milk. Grind the residue with two cups of warm water and strain to extract thin coconut milk.

3. Heat the oil in a pressure cooker. Add the cinnamon, cloves and green cardamoms and sauté till fragrant. Add the onions and green chillies and sauté till the onions are transparent.

4. Add the ginger-garlic paste and sauté over low heat for two to three minutes. Add the marinated mutton and sauté for ten minutes over low heat.

5. Add the thin coconut milk and secure the lid of the pressure cooker. Cook till the pressure is released five to six times (five to six whistles).

6. Remove the lid when the pressure has reduced completely. Stir in the thick coconut milk and adjust salt. Simmer for five minutes.

7. Garnish with the fresh coriander and serve hot.

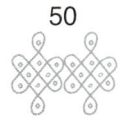

Tamil Nadu

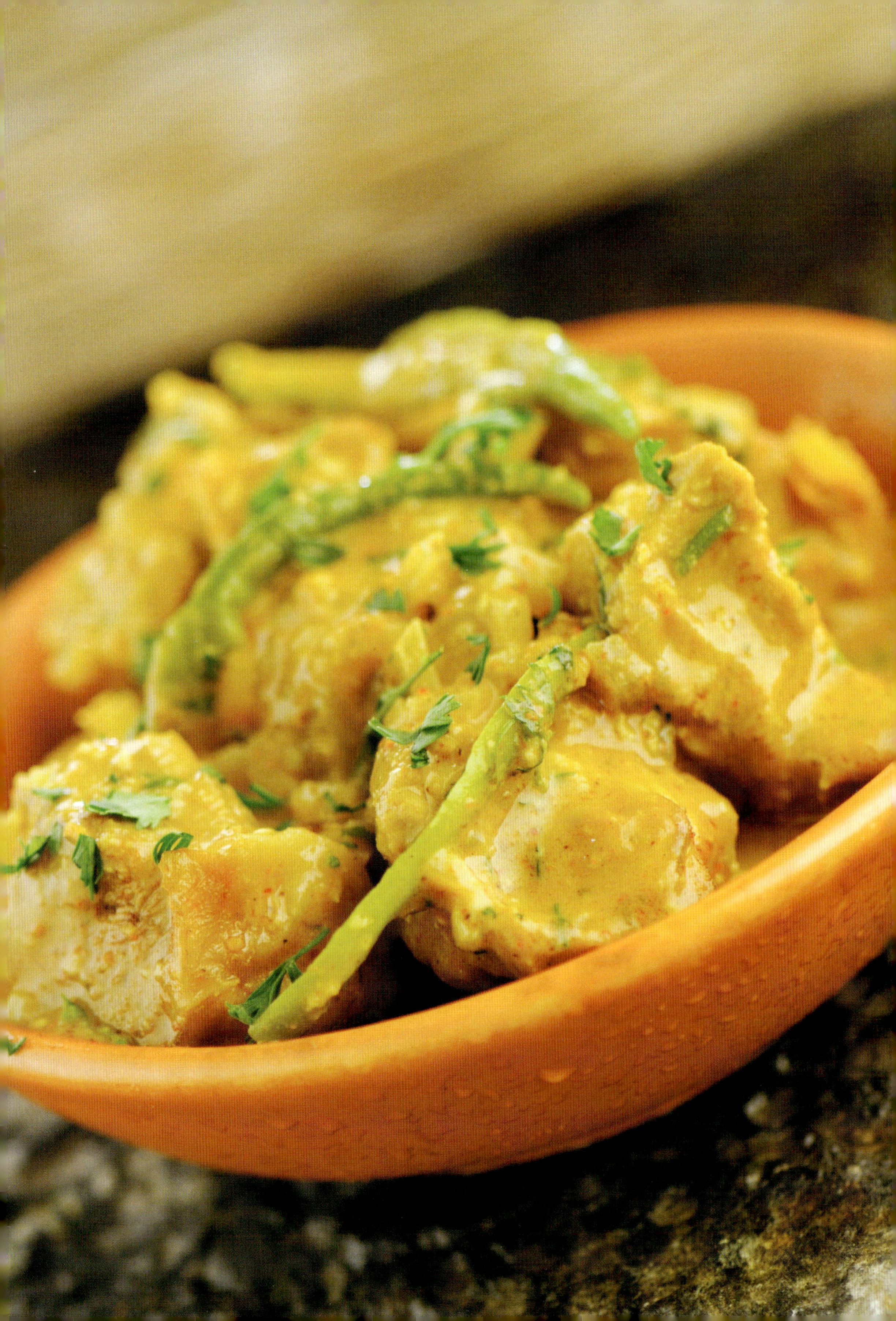

IGGARU ROYYA

Coastal Kerala prawn curry

Ingredients

36 (350 grams) medium prawns

5 tablespoons oil

1 cup grated coconut

8 dried red chillies, broken into bits

1 teaspoon cumin seeds

½ teaspoon fenugreek seeds

10-12 black peppercorns

2 medium onions, chopped

2 teaspoons ginger paste

2 teaspoons garlic paste

2 medium tomatoes, chopped

Salt to taste

10-12 curry leaves

2 tablespoons chopped fresh coriander

| *Coconut and pepper give this prawn curry the quintessential flavours of the spice coast.* |

Method

1. Wash, peel and devein the prawns and pat them dry.

2. Heat two tablespoons of oil in a *kadai* and sauté the coconut, red chillies, cumin seeds, fenugreek seeds and peppercorns till the coconut turns light brown. Cool and grind to a coarse paste.

3. Heat the remaining oil in the same *kadai*; add the onions and sauté till golden brown. Add the ginger paste and garlic paste and sauté till all the moisture evaporates. Add the ground paste and stir well.

4. Add the tomatoes, salt and curry leaves, and sauté over low heat for three to four minutes.

5. Add the prawns, mix well and cook till the prawns are tender. Garnish with the fresh coriander and serve hot.

Chef's Tip
Traditionally, this is a thick curry; but if you want to serve it with rice, thin the curry down with a little water.

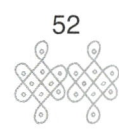

Kerala

ANDHRA CHILLI CHICKEN

Ingredients

1 medium (800 grams) chicken
8-10 dried red chillies
Salt to taste
4 tablespoons lemon juice
2 one-inch pieces of ginger
6-8 garlic cloves
8-10 curry leaves
2 tablespoons rice
½ cup yogurt
¼ cup oil
¼ cup refined flour
2 tablespoons chopped fresh coriander

I think this is as good as tandoori chicken when it comes to chicken dish!

Method

1. Cut the chicken into four – two leg and two breast pieces. Make four to five half-inch deep slits on the chicken pieces. Rub the salt and two tablespoons of lemon juice all over the chicken and set aside.

2. Grind the ginger, garlic, curry leaves, red chillies and rice with the remaining lemon juice to a smooth paste. Add the paste to the yogurt and whisk well till smooth. Add salt to taste. Spread the yogurt mixture liberally over the chicken and leave to marinate for four to six hours, preferably in a refrigerator.

3. Heat the oil in a pan; roll the marinated chicken in the flour, shake off excess flour and add to the pan. Cook for one minute, turn over the chicken pieces and cook for another minute.

4. Lower the heat and cook for five to six minutes, turning the chicken frequently to cook evenly on all sides.

5. Drain and transfer the chicken to a shallow pan and keep warm over medium heat. Sprinkle the fresh coriander and two tablespoons of water over the chicken and cover with a tight-fitting lid. Lower the heat and cook for five minutes over low heat, or until the chicken is completely cooked. Serve hot.

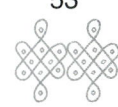

Andhra Pradesh

NANDU MILAGU KOZHAMBU
Peppery crab curry

Ingredients
4 medium crabs (approximately 1 kilogram)
20-25 black peppercorns
2 teaspoons red chilli powder
2 teaspoons coriander powder
1 teaspoon cumin powder
1 tablespoon Tamarind Pulp (page 103)
1 cup grated coconut
2 teaspoons poppy seeds
4 tablespoons oil
1 large onion, chopped
2 teaspoons garlic paste
10-12 curry leaves
Salt to taste
½ teaspoon mustard seeds

> Crabs are best when cooked 'just so' as they start to disintegrate if overcooked. Keep checking at regular intervals during the cooking process.

Method
1. Clean the crabs thoroughly under running water. Cut each crab into two halves through the centre. Crack the claws lightly.

2. Lightly roast and pound the peppercorns to a coarse powder.

3. Mix the chilli powder, coriander powder and cumin powder into the tamarind pulp.

4. Soak the coconut and poppy seeds in half a cup of hot water for fifteen minutes. Grind to a smooth paste.

5. Heat two tablespoons of oil in a deep pan; add the onion and sauté till light brown. Add the garlic paste and sauté for half a minute. Add the curry leaves and continue to sauté for another minute.

6. Add the tamarind pulp mixture and cook over medium heat for about five minutes.

7. Add the crabs and the pounded peppercorns and mix well. Lower the heat and simmer for another five minutes.

8. Finally, add the coconut paste and salt to taste. Add one cup of water and cook till the crabs are cooked and the curry thickens.

9. Heat the remaining oil and add the mustard seeds. When they begin to splutter, pour them over the crab curry and cover immediately. Serve with steamed rice.

Chef's Tip
It is advisable to purchase live crabs to ensure freshness. Get your fishmonger to cut them. Do not boil or precook the crabs.

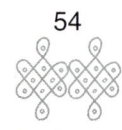

Tamil Nadu

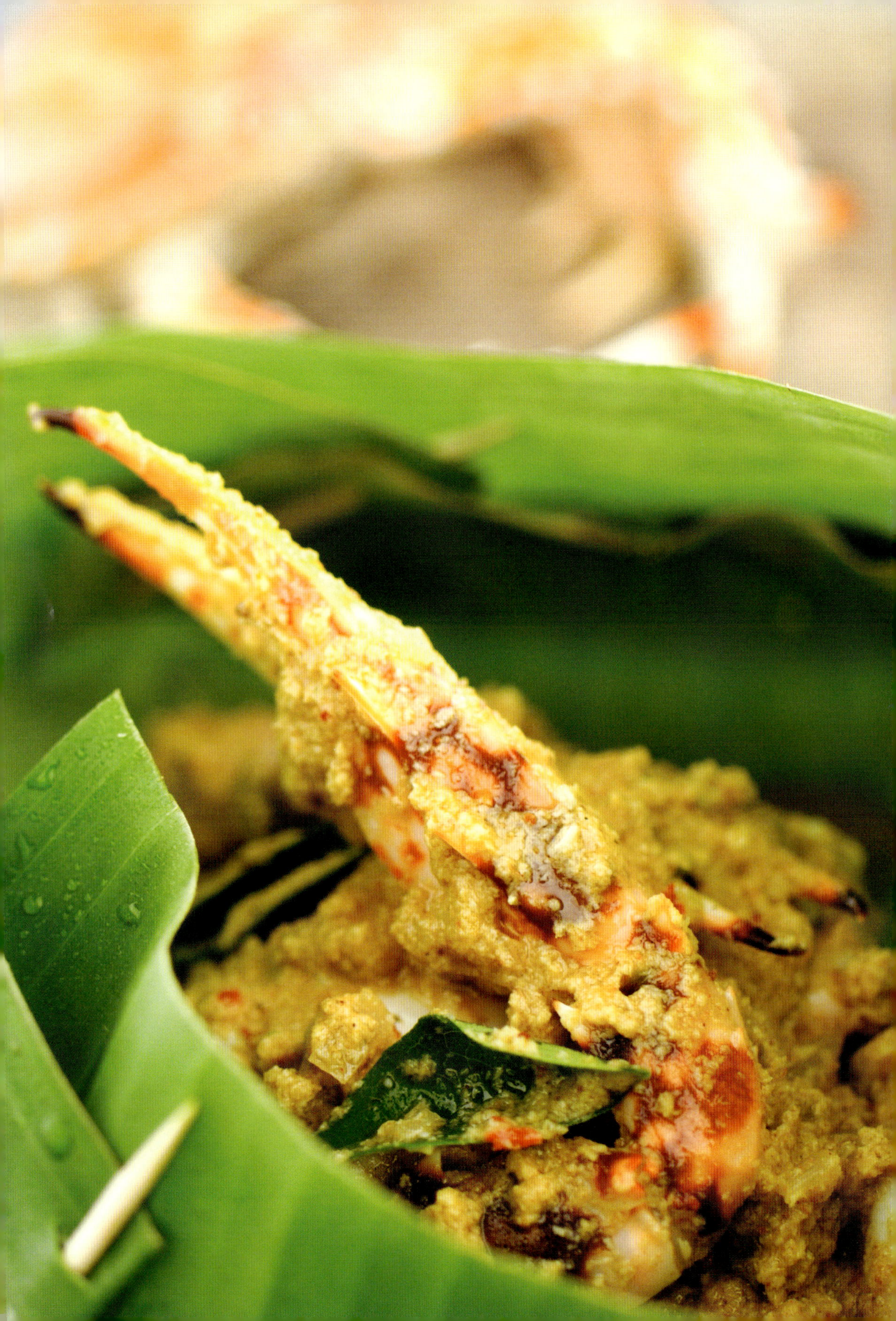

CHETTINAD KOZHI MILAGU VARUVAL
Chettinad peppery chicken

Ingredients

800 grams boneless chicken, cut into small pieces

20 black peppercorns, crushed

2 tablespoons oil

½ teaspoon mustard seeds

1 inch ginger, chopped

7-8 garlic cloves, chopped

2 medium onions, chopped

12 curry leaves

1 teaspoon turmeric powder

1 teaspoon red chilli powder

1 teaspoon coriander powder

3 medium tomatoes, chopped

Salt to taste

Method

1. Heat the oil in a deep pan; add the mustard seeds and when they begin to splutter, add the ginger, garlic and onions and sauté till golden brown.

2. Add the curry leaves, turmeric powder, chilli powder, coriander powder and crushed peppercorns and sauté for a minute.

3. Add the tomatoes and salt to taste and sauté till the tomatoes soften.

4. Stir in the chicken, cover and simmer till the chicken is cooked and the mixture is almost dry, stirring occasionally. You can sprinkle a little water if necessary to prevent scorching. Serve hot.

Dominated by black pepper, this is a fiery, sample of Chettinad cuisine.

Tamil Nadu

FISH MOILEE

Fish in a mild coconut curry

Ingredients

600 grams *rohu*
Salt to taste
2 teaspoons lemon juice
1 tablespoon oil
½ teaspoon mustard seeds
10 curry leaves
2 medium onions, chopped
2 teaspoons ginger paste
2 teaspoons garlic paste
3 green chillies, slit
1 teaspoon turmeric powder
1½ cups Thick Coconut Milk (page 103)

In days gone by, Kerala had a flourishing trade with the Portuguese. Moilee is a corruption of the Portuguese 'molho' or Spanish 'mole', both of which mean sauce. This moilee is delicately spiced, enriched with coconut milk and tastes superb with appam.

Method

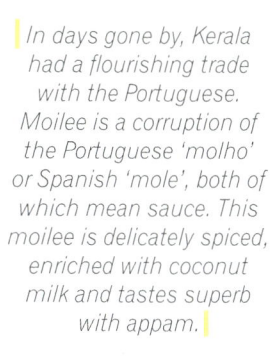

1. Clean, wash and cut the fish into one-inch thick slices. Rub a little salt and lemon juice over the fish and set aside for fifteen minutes.

2. Heat the oil in a *kadai* and add the mustard seeds. When they begin to splutter, add the curry leaves and sauté for ten seconds. Add the onions and cook until soft and translucent.

3. Add the ginger paste, garlic paste, green chillies, turmeric powder and the fish. Cook over high heat for half a minute.

4. Add the coconut milk and salt, and cook, covered, over low heat for about ten minutes.

5. Serve hot with steamed rice.

Kerala

ERATCHI OLATHIYATHU
Mutton curry

Ingredients

500 grams mutton on the bone, cut into 1½-inch pieces

1 tablespoon red chilli powder

1 tablespoon coriander powder

Salt to taste

1 teaspoon fennel seeds

4-5 black peppercorns

½ cup oil

2 medium onions, sliced

2 green chillies, slit

10-12 curry leaves

2 teaspoons ginger paste

2 teaspoons garlic paste

1 medium tomato, chopped

¼ dried coconut, cut into thin strips

Malayali food is normally spicy but this mutton dish with chewy pieces of dried coconut does not bombard the senses. The fennel will surprise you, and that probably is the blanket on the spice!

Method

1. Marinate the mutton in a mixture of chilli powder, coriander powder and salt for about half an hour. Roast and coarsely pound the fennel seeds and peppercorns.

2. Heat the oil in a deep pan; add the onions and green chillies and sauté till the onions are lightly browned. Add the curry leaves and sauté for half a minute. Add the ginger paste and garlic paste and sauté for ten minutes over low heat.

3. Add the mutton and sauté for ten minutes. Add the tomato and cook till soft.

4. Add one cup of water and bring the mixture to a boil. Cover the pan, lower the heat and cook till the mutton is almost tender, adding another cup of water if required.

5. Add the dried coconut strips and cook till the mutton is tender.

6. Garnish with the coarsely pounded fennel and peppercorns and serve hot.

Chef's Tip
Get your butcher to cut the mutton, so that there are no splinters of bone.

Kerala

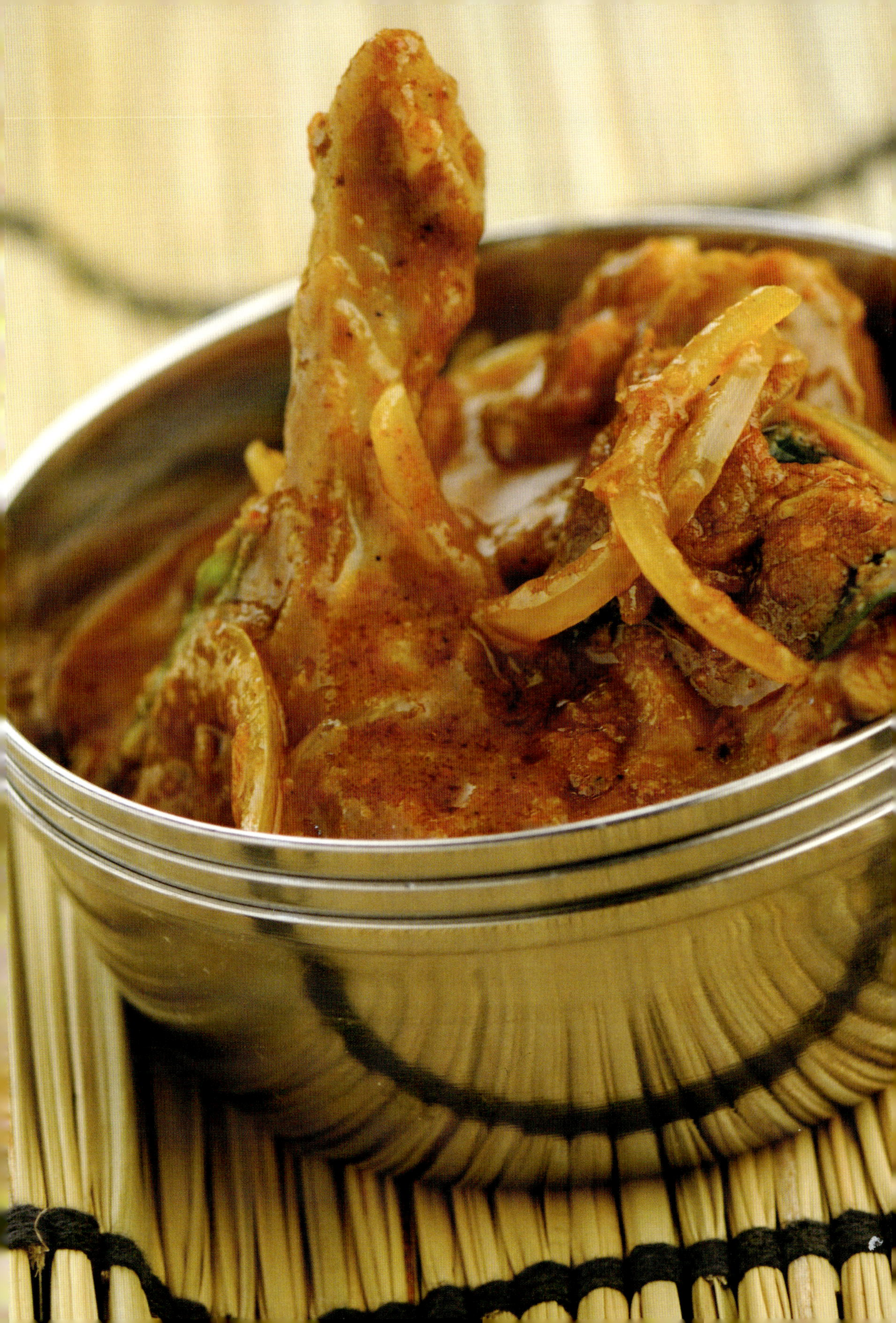

KOZHI THENGAI KOZHAMBU
Chicken in a coconut curry

Ingredients

1 medium chicken (800 grams)

½ teaspoon turmeric powder

Salt to taste

2 tablespoons oil

2 star anise

2 bay leaves

10-12 curry leaves

Masala

2 tablespoons oil

1 cup grated coconut

25 shallots, peeled

1 inch ginger, chopped

12 garlic cloves, chopped

10 green chillies, chopped

2 dried red chillies, broken into bits

2 tablespoons coriander seeds

Method

1. Clean and cut the chicken into medium-sized pieces (approximately twenty to twenty-four pieces). Rub in the turmeric powder and a little salt.

2. Heat two tablespoons of oil and fry the ingredients for the *masala* till light brown. Cool and grind to a smooth paste with a little water.

3. Heat the oil in a deep pan; add the star anise and bay leaves and sauté for half a minute.

4. Add the curry leaves and the marinated chicken. Sauté over high heat to seal the juices of the chicken.

5. Add the *masala* paste and mix thoroughly. Add one and a half cups of water and simmer till the chicken is almost cooked.

6. Add salt to taste, stir well and simmer till the chicken is tender and the gravy thickens.

Chef's Tip
Instead of using grated coconut, try making the dish with just coconut milk – the curry will be smoother and have a richer flavour.

This chicken coconut curry from Tamil Nadu has two distinct features: loads of green chillies and their heat neutralised with plenty of coconut! The shallots add a hint of sweetness.

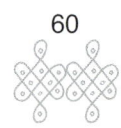

Tamil Nadu

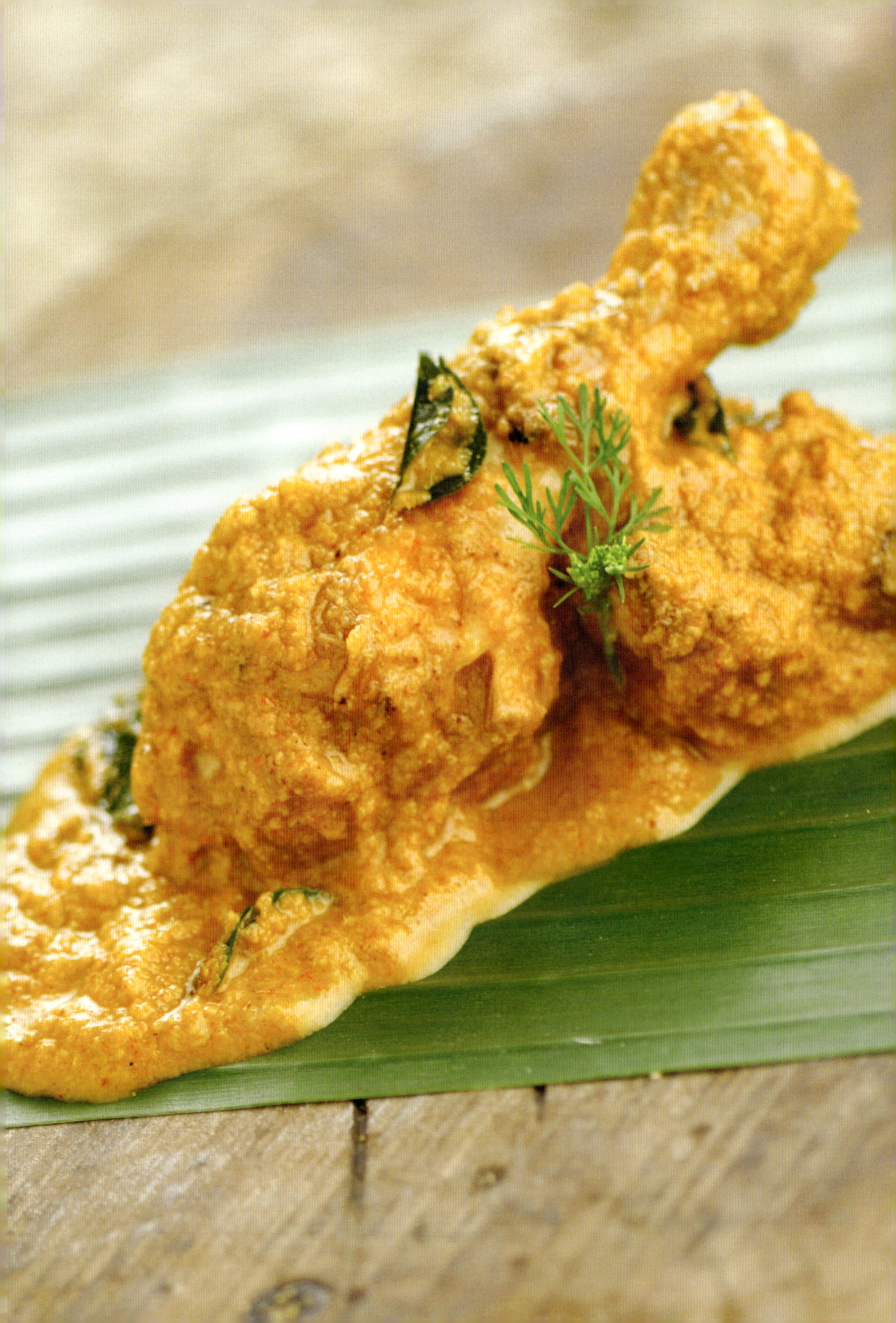

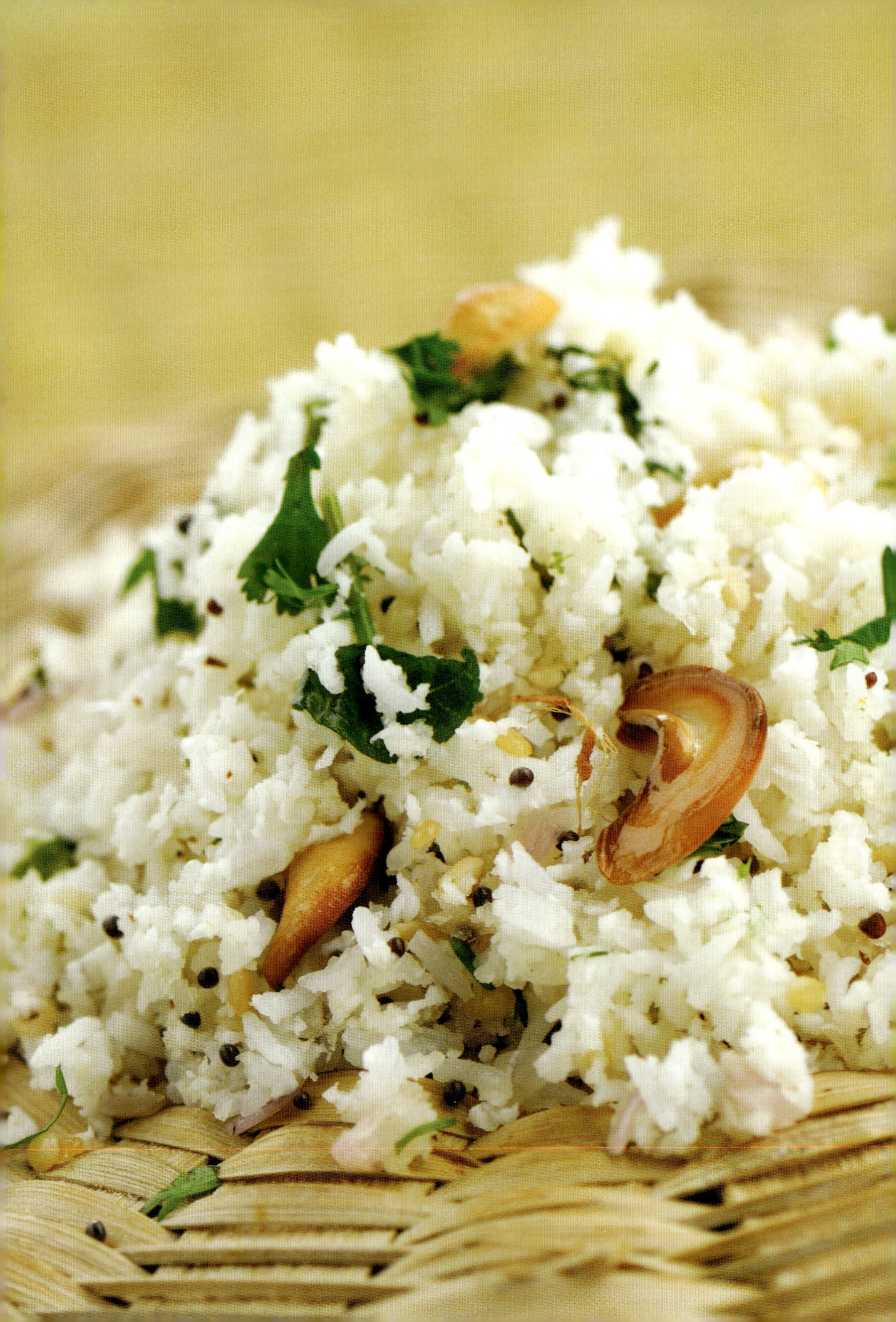

RICE AND BREAD

Bisi Bele Hulianna 64

Kaikari Biryani 66

Chitranna 68

Kongunadu Eratchi Biryani 70

Bakala Bhaat 72

Arumainayagam Chitarannam 74

Puliodharai 75

Thengai Sadham 76

Appam 78

Neer Dosa 79

BISI BELE HULIANNA
Masala rice

Ingredients
1½ cups rice, soaked
¾ cup split pigeon peas, soaked
1½ lemon-sized balls tamarind
5 tablespoons oil
1 medium onion, sliced
3-4 green chillies, slit
8-10 shallots, peeled
10-12 curry leaves
½ teaspoon turmeric powder
3 medium tomatoes, quartered
¼ teaspoon asafoetida
½ teaspoon red chilli powder
Salt to taste
½ teaspoon mustard seeds
2 dried red chillies, broken into bits
4 tablespoons pure ghee
10-12 cashew nuts

Hulianna Masala
¼ cup split Bengal gram
2 tablespoons skinless split black gram
4 green cardamoms
4 cloves
1 inch cinnamon
1 teaspoon fenugreek seeds
1 teaspoon cumin seeds
4 dried red chillies

Method

1. Soak the tamarind in one cup of warm water for half an hour. Extract the pulp, strain and set aside.

2. Dry-roast the *hulianna masala* ingredients individually on a *tawa*. Cool, mix and grind to a coarse powder.

3. Heat three tablespoons of oil in a pressure cooker and sauté the onion till it turns translucent. Add the green chillies, shallots and sauté for a minute. Stir in the curry leaves and turmeric powder.

4. Add the soaked rice and split pigeon peas along with five cups of water and bring to a boil, stirring occasionally.

5. Add the tomatoes, asafoetida, chilli powder and salt. Stir well and add the powdered *hulianna masala*. Cover and cook till the pressure is released three to four times (three to four whistles).

6. Remove the lid when the pressure reduces completely and stir well. Check the consistency - if it is too dry, add a little warm water.

7. Heat the remaining oil and add the mustard seeds and red chillies. When the mustard seeds begin to splutter, pour the spices over the rice mixture and stir.

8. Heat the ghee in a pan and fry the cashew nuts till light brown and add to the rice. Mix well and serve hot.

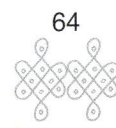

Karnataka

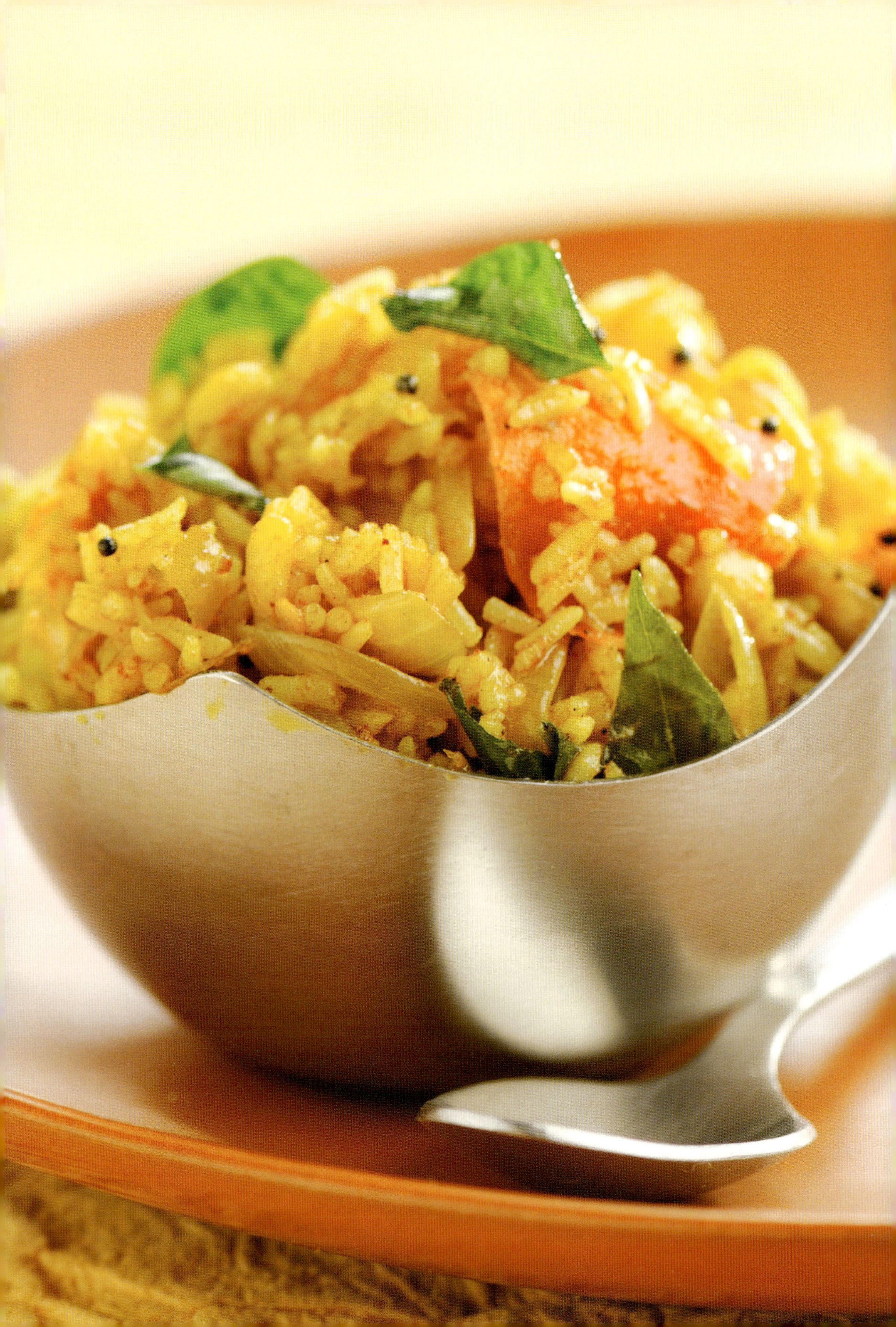

KAIKARI BIRYANI
Vegetable biryani

Ingredients

1½ cups long-grained rice, soaked

1 medium tomato, seeded and cubed

1 medium green capsicum, seeded and cubed

1 medium carrot, cubed

2 medium potatoes, cubed

10 French beans, cut into ½-inch pieces

¼ small cauliflower, separated into small florets

¼ cup shelled green peas

8 tablespoons oil

2 medium onions, chopped

10-12 curry leaves

4 green chillies, slit

Salt to taste

¼ cup chopped fresh coriander leaves

8-10 fresh mint leaves, roughly torn

1 tablespoon lemon juice

Method

1. For the *masala paste*, heat two tablespoons of oil in a small pan or on a *tawa* and fry all the *masala* ingredients till light brown. Cool and grind to a smooth paste with a little water.

2. Dry-roast all the ingredients for the *garam masala* for two to three minutes and pound into a coarse powder.

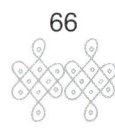

Kerala

Masala Paste

2 tablespoons oil

10-12 garlic cloves, roughly chopped

1 inch ginger, roughly chopped

¼ cup grated coconut

4 dried red chillies

2 tablespoons coriander seeds

1 teaspoon cumin seeds

1 tablespoon poppy seeds

2 tablespoons fennel seeds

Garam Masala

½ inch cinnamon

2 cloves

2 green cardamoms

2 blades of mace

1 star anise

10-12 black peppercorns

A small pinch of nutmeg powder

3. Heat the remaining oil in a pan and sauté the onions till golden brown. Add the curry leaves, green chillies and *masala* paste and sauté till the oil separates. Add the tomato and cook over high heat till the moisture evaporates. Stir in all the remaining vegetables and cook for a couple of minutes over high heat.

4. Drain the rice well and add to the vegetable mixture with salt to taste. Add three and a half cups of hot water and bring to a boil over high heat. Lower the heat to medium, cover and cook, stirring occasionally, till the rice is almost cooked.

5. Sprinkle the chopped coriander and mint, freshly pounded *garam masala* powder and lemon juice. Stir well and cover with a tight-fitting lid.

6. Place the pan on hot charcoals for about ten minutes. Uncover the pan when ready to serve.

Kaikari (vegetables in Malayalam) are an important ingredient in this flavourful and spicy South Indian pulao which is fashioned on the iconic Hyderabadi biryani.

Chef's Tip
Traditionally Jeeraga Samba rice is used to make this *biryani*.
However, you can use any other long-grained rice.

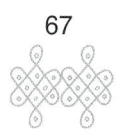

CHITRANNA

Lemon rice

Ingredients

1½ cups rice, soaked
Salt to taste
1 tablespoon oil
1 teaspoon mustard seeds
A pinch of asafoetida
6-8 curry leaves
½ teaspoon ginger paste
1 green chilli, finely chopped
2 dried red chillies, broken into bits
7-8 cashew nuts, split and lightly fried
1 teaspoon skinless split black gram
1 teaspoon split Bengal gram
½ teaspoon turmeric powder
2 tablespoons lemon juice
2 tablespoons chopped fresh coriander

Method

1. Drain and cook the soaked rice in six cups of boiling, salted water until almost done. Drain and set aside.

2. Heat the oil in a *kadai*; add the mustard seeds. When they begin to splutter, add the asafoetida, curry leaves, ginger paste, green chilli, red chillies, cashew nuts, split black gram, split Bengal gram and turmeric powder. Sauté till the lentils are lightly browned.

3. Add the lemon juice, salt and one tablespoon of water. Simmer for two to three minutes.

4. Add the rice and toss to mix. Cover and cook till the rice is heated through.

5. Serve hot, garnished with the chopped coriander.

This is the famous lemon rice of the south. You can dress it up by adding beetroot, capsicum, onion or peanuts.

Karnataka

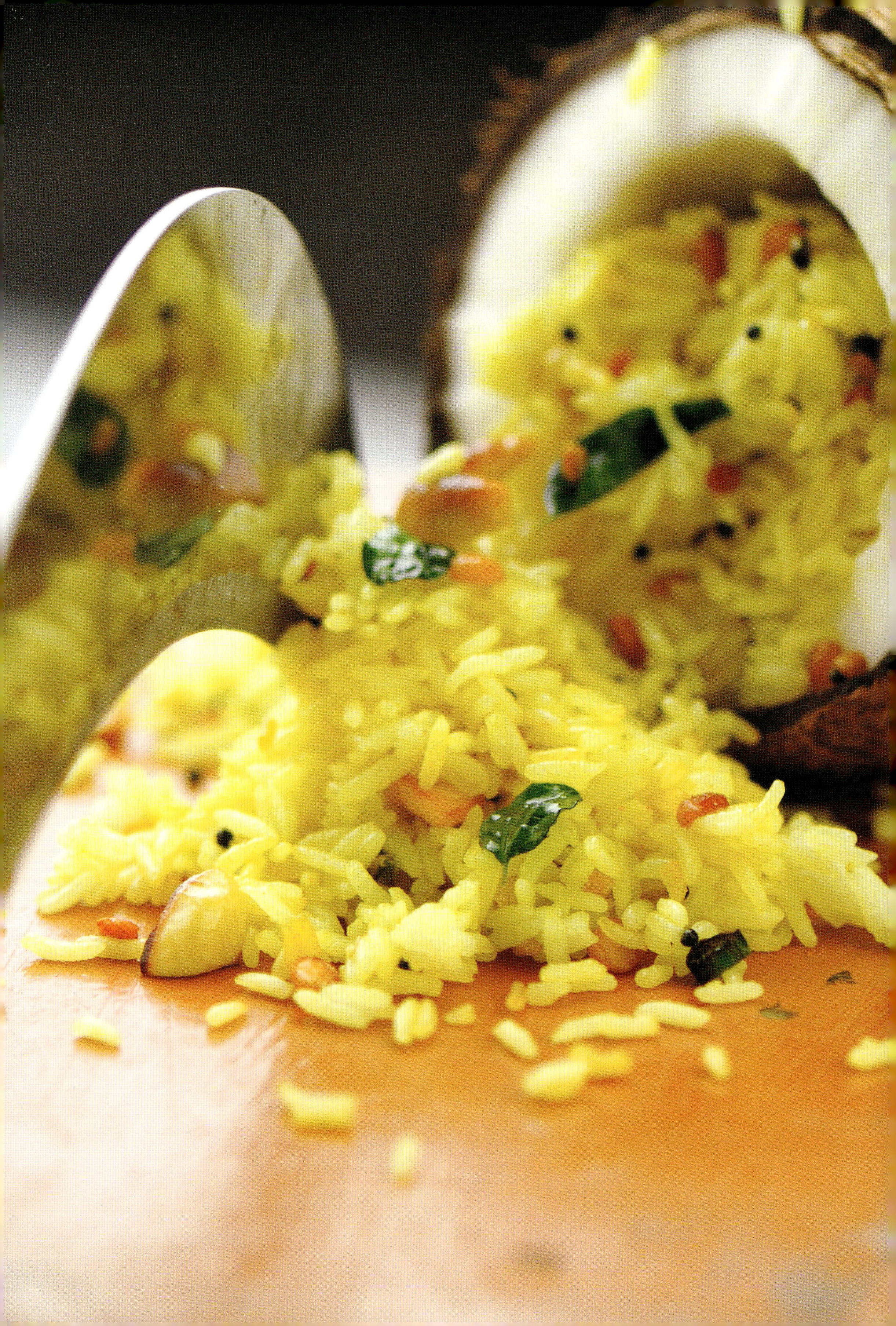

KONGUNADU ERATCHI BIRYANI

Mutton biryani

Ingredients

500 grams mutton on the bone, cut into ½-inch pieces

1½ cups long-grained rice, soaked

½ teaspoon turmeric powder

Salt to taste

4 tablespoons oil + for deep-frying

2 onions, sliced thinly

½ cup grated coconut

8-10 black peppercorns

8 dried red chillies

1 tablespoon cumin seeds

1 tablespoon fennel seeds

2 tablespoons coriander seeds

1 tablespoon poppy seeds

1 inch ginger

12 garlic cloves

½ cup yogurt

Method

1. Rub the turmeric powder and salt into the mutton and set aside for fifteen minutes.

2. Heat sufficient oil in a *kadai* and deep-fry the onions till golden brown. Drain on absorbent paper.

3. Dry-roast the coconut, peppercorns, red chillies, cumin seeds, fennel seeds, coriander seeds, poppy seeds, ginger and garlic, one by one, till fragrant. Cool and grind to a smooth paste with the yogurt.

4. Wash the mutton thoroughly and parboil in four cups of water. Drain and reserve both the meat and the water.

5. Heat four tablespoons of oil in a heavy-bottomed *handi*; add the bay leaves, cardamoms, cinnamon, star anise, cloves, mace and green chillies and sauté till fragrant.

6. Add the shallots and sauté till light brown. Add the mutton and stir-fry over high heat till the edges start browning. Add the tomatoes and stir.

7. Add the ground paste, lower the heat and sauté till the oil separates. Add two cups of the reserved mutton stock and cook over low heat for ten minutes.

2 bay leaves

4 green cardamoms

1 inch cinnamon

1 star anise

2 cloves

1 blade of mace

6 green chillies, slit

10-12 shallots, peeled

2 medium tomatoes, chopped

2 tablespoons chopped fresh mint

3 tablespoons chopped fresh coriander

1 tablespoon lemon juice

8. Add the soaked rice, the remaining mutton stock and salt to taste. Stir well and cook till the rice is three-fourths done.

9. Sprinkle the browned onions, chopped mint and coriander over the rice and drizzle with the lemon juice. Cover the *handi* with a tight-fitting lid and place on hot charcoals, with a few burning charcoals on the lid as well. Cook for ten to fifteen minutes.

10. Remove the lid when ready to serve.

Chef's Tip
You can make this *biryani* with chicken, boiled eggs or minced mutton *kofte*.
Traditionally, Jeeraga Samba rice is used for this *biryani*, but you can use any long-grained rice.

This mutton biryani is an example of the centuries-old Kongunadu cuisine from the central part of South India, where the Kongunadu kingdom once held sway.

Tamil Nadu

BAKALA BHAAT
Yogurt or "curd" rice

Ingredients
1½ cups rice (Kolam)
1 cup yogurt
½ cup milk
Salt to taste
2 tablespoons oil
1 teaspoon mustard seeds
¼ teaspoon asafoetida
1 dried red chilli, broken into bits
8-10 curry leaves
1 inch ginger, chopped
4 green chillies, chopped
¼ cup fresh cream
1 medium cucumber, seeds removed and grated
1 medium carrot, grated

Method

1. Boil the rice in four and a half cups of water and slightly overcook it. Drain well and set aside to cool. When it reaches room temperature, add the milk and salt to taste.

2. Heat the oil in a small pan; add the mustard seeds, asafoetida, red chilli and curry leaves. When the seeds begin to splutter, add the ginger and green chillies and sauté for half a minute. Add to the rice.

3. Stir in the yogurt and cream and chill in a refrigerator.

4. Squeeze out the excess water from the cucumber. Garnish the rice with the cucumber and carrot and serve.

Chef's Tip
If you are preparing *bakala bhaat* much in advance of serving, reduce the quantity of yogurt and increase the quantity of milk. This will prevent the rice from becoming too sour.

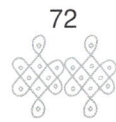

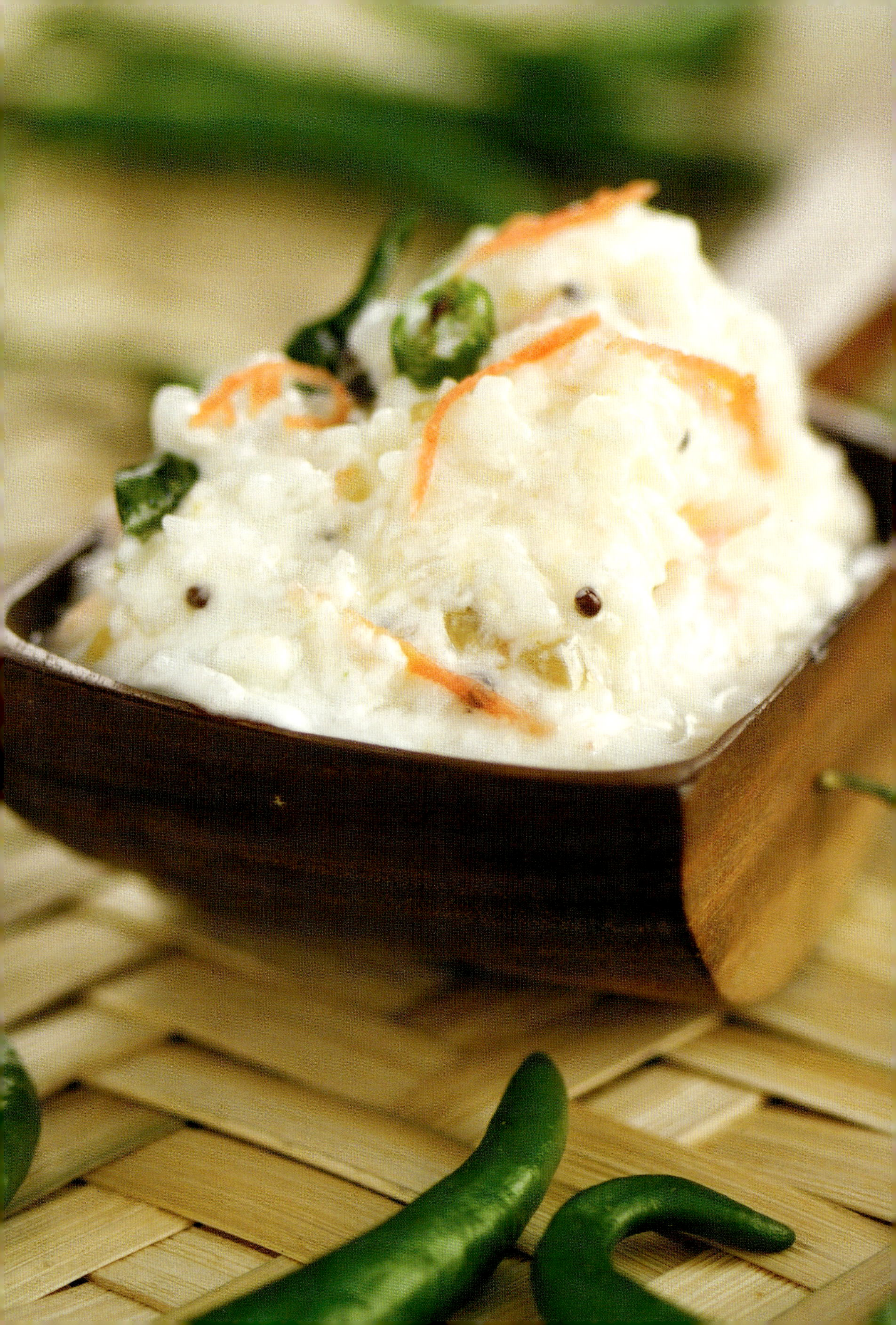

ARUMAINAYAGAM CHITARANNAM

Rice and prawns tossed in light spices

Ingredients

1½ cups rice, soaked
35 (260 grams) small prawns
Salt to taste
½ teaspoon turmeric powder
1 teaspoon red chilli powder
2 tablespoons oil
1 teaspoon cumin seeds
2 medium onions, chopped
1 teaspoon ginger paste
1 teaspoon garlic paste
8-10 black peppercorns
5-6 curry leaves
1 green cardamom
2 tablespoons chopped fresh coriander

Method

1. Peel and devein the prawns. Marinate them in a mixture of salt, turmeric powder and chilli powder for twenty minutes.

2. Heat the oil in a heavy-bottomed pan and fry the prawns till tender. Drain and set aside.

3. To the same oil, add the cumin seeds. When they begin to change colour, add the onions, ginger paste, garlic paste, peppercorns and curry leaves, and sauté till the onions soften. Add the green cardamom and stir.

4. Add the soaked rice and sauté until the rice becomes translucent.

5. Add three cups of hot water, salt and the prawns. Stir and bring to a boil.

6. Lower the heat and cook, covered, for at least twenty minutes or till the rice is cooked. Garnish with the chopped coriander and serve hot.

Tamil Nadu

PULIODHARAI

Tamarind rice

Ingredients

1½ cups rice
6 tablespoons oil
2 lemon-sized balls of tamarind
½ cup raw peanuts
¼ cup white sesame seeds
1 teaspoon mustard seeds
2 dried red chillies
6-8 curry leaves
½ teaspoon turmeric powder
Salt to taste

Masala

2 tablespoons split Bengal gram
1 tablespoon skinless split black gram
1 teaspoon fenugreek seeds
10 dried red chillies
¼ teaspoon asafoetida
6-8 curry leaves

Method

1. Boil the rice in five cups of water till three-fourth done. Drain and mix in two tablespoons of oil and set aside to cool.

2. Soak the tamarind in one cup of warm water, extract the pulp and set aside.

3. Heat two tablespoons of oil and sauté the ingredients for the *masala*. Cool and grind to a coarse powder.

4. Soak the peanuts for five minutes and drain. Dry-roast the sesame seeds over medium heat, cool and pound to a coarse powder.

5. Heat the remaining oil in a deep pan; add the mustard seeds, red chillies and curry leaves. When the mustard seeds begin to splutter, add the peanuts and sauté till fragrant.

6. Add the tamarind pulp and cook for a few minutes. Add the *masala* powder and turmeric powder and bring to a boil. Lower heat and simmer till fragrant.

7. Add the salt and mix well. Stir frequently till the oil separates and the mixture reduces to a fairly thick consistency.

8. Add the cooled rice and toss to mix well. Sprinkle the sesame powder and serve immediately.

Chef's Tip

You can make the tamarind mixture in a larger quantity and store it in a refrigerator. Mix with hot rice whenever required. Use extra oil for a longer shelf-life. This dish is traditionally cooked in a stone vessel to enhance the flavour.

Tamil Nadu

THENGAI SADHAM
Coconut rice

Ingredients

1 cup grated coconut

1½ cups rice, soaked

1 tablespoon pure ghee

6-8 cashew nuts

4 tablespoons oil

½ teaspoon mustard seeds

1 teaspoon skinless split black gram

2 dried red chillies, broken into two

10-12 curry leaves

1 medium onion, finely chopped

2 green chillies, finely chopped

1 inch ginger, finely chopped

Salt to taste

2 tablespoons chopped fresh coriander

1 teaspoon coconut oil (optional)

Method

1. Boil sufficient water in a deep pan and cook the rice, stirring frequently till almost done. Drain and spread out on a flat plate to cool.

2. Heat the ghee in a small pan and stir-fry the cashew nuts till light brown and set aside.

3. Heat the oil in a *kadai* and add the mustard seeds. When they begin to splutter, add the split black gram, red chillies and curry leaves and sauté for a few seconds.

4. Add the onion, green chillies and ginger, and sauté for two to three minutes, or until the onion is translucent. Add the coconut and cook over medium heat for two minutes. Add the cooked rice, salt and chopped coriander and toss well to mix. Cook till the rice is heated through.

5. Drizzle with the coconut oil and mix lightly. Serve hot, garnished with the fried cashew nuts.

An ideal candidate for the lunch box. You can also use leftover rice with fresh coconut to make this dish.

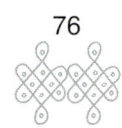

Tamil Nadu

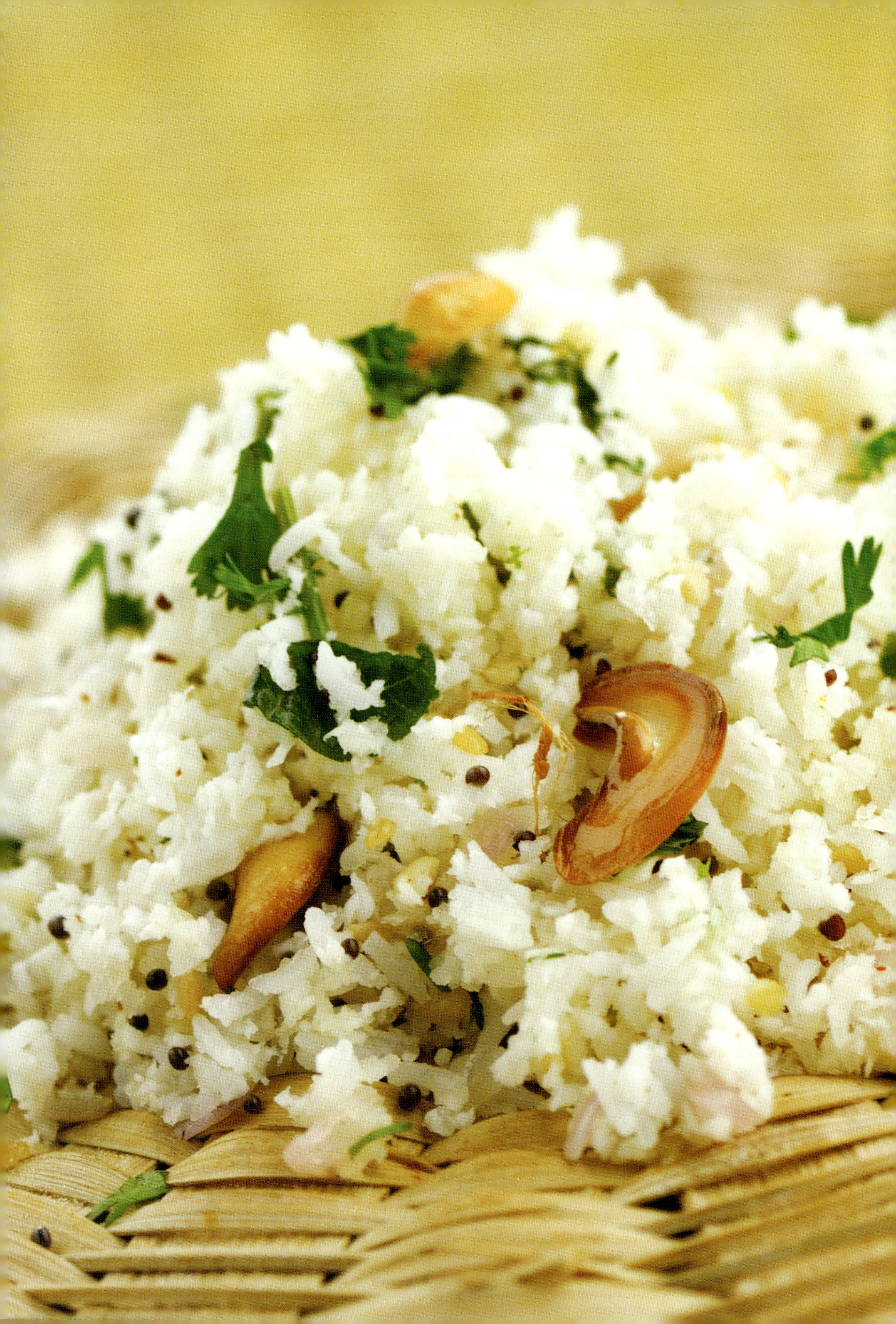

APPAM
Coconut-flavoured rice bread

Ingredients
1 cup rice
1 cup parboiled rice
¼ cup coconut water
Salt to taste
¾ cup grated coconut
¼ teaspoon baking powder
Oil to grease the *appam tawa*

Method

1. Soak both the varieties of rice together in four cups of water for two to three hours. Drain and grind to a smooth paste adding the coconut water, as required.

2. Add the salt, stir well and set aside in a warm place to ferment for at least thirty-six hours.

3. Soak the grated coconut in one and a half cups of warm water; grind and extract thick milk. Add the coconut milk to the fermented batter to dilute it to a thick and creamy consistency. Mix in the baking powder and adjust the salt.

4. Heat an *appam tawa*; brush it with a little oil. Pour in one ladleful of batter and tilt the *kadai* all round to spread the batter. The edges should be thin and the excess batter should collect in the centre at the bottom.

5. Cover with a thick heavy lid and cook over medium heat for two to thee minutes. Check to see if the sides start leaving the *tawa*. The edges of the *appam* should be crisp and thin and the centre soft and spongy.

6. Serve hot with Kaikari Ishtew (page 37).

| *Appam turn out spongy if the batter has been allowed to ferment well.*

Chef's Tips
- Traditionally fresh toddy is used to ferment *appam* batter. In the above recipe, the coconut water acts as the fermenting agent.
- A special cast iron *appam tawa* is used to make *appam*. However, you may use a small non-stick *kadai*.

Kerala

NEER DOSA

Instant rice pancakes

Ingredients
2 cups rice
Salt to taste
Oil for shallow-frying

Method

1. Pick over, wash and soak rice in four cups of water for twelve hours. Drain and grind to a fine paste with half a cup of water.

2. Add salt and three and a half cups of water to make a batter of pouring consistency.

3. Heat the *dosa tawa* and pour just enough oil to grease it.

4. Stir the batter and pour a ladleful of batter onto the *tawa* starting from the outer edge and moving towards the centre so that it spreads in a thin, even layer. Do not use the ladle to spread it. Cover and cook for ten to fifteen seconds.

5. Remove the *dosa* carefully, fold into a triangle and serve immediately.

Karnataka

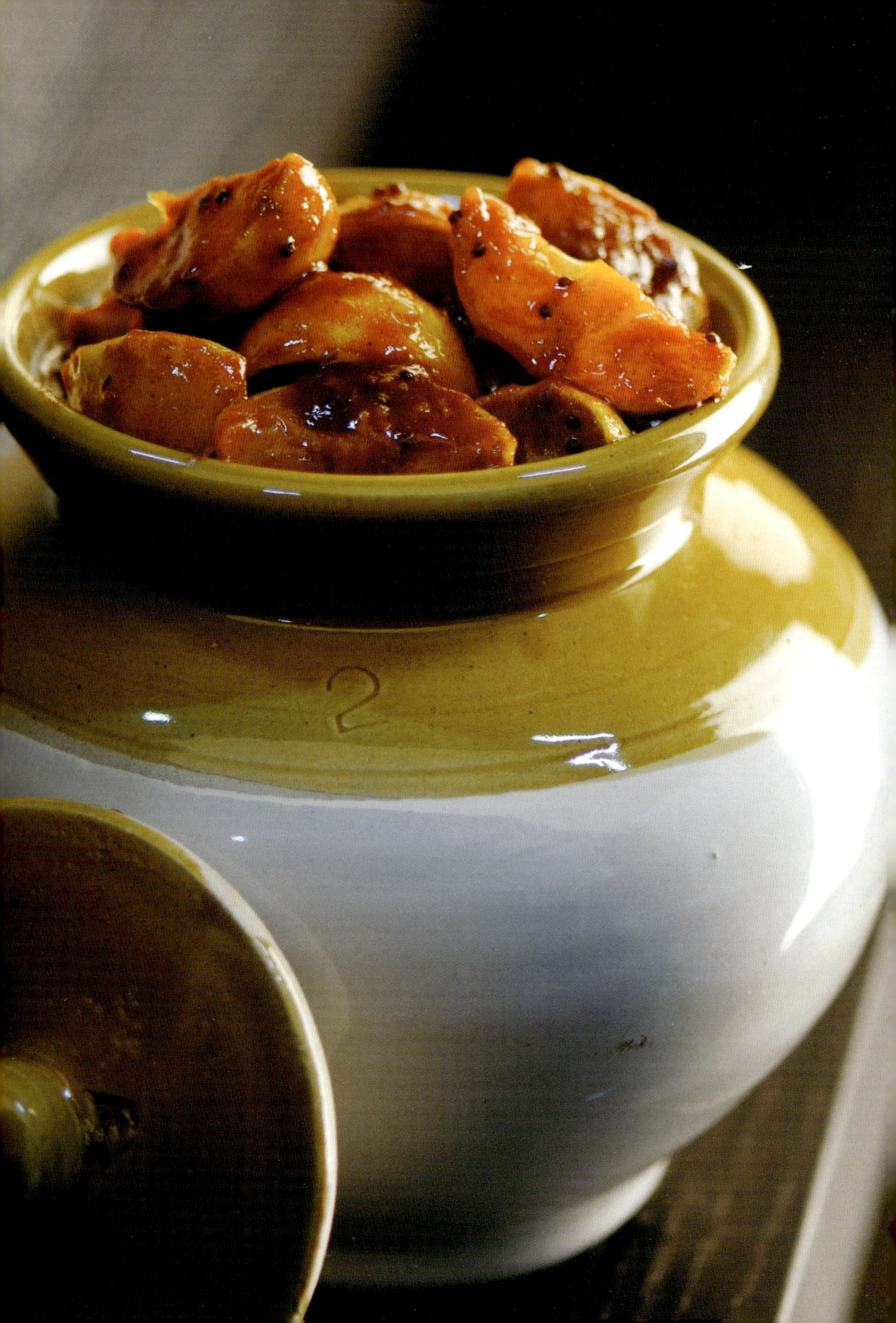

ACCOMPANIMENTS

Artekai Pappu 82

Paruppu Thuvayal 83

Inji-Thakkali Thuvayal 84

Birakai Chutney 84

Thakkali Pachadi 85

Vendakkai Pachadi 85

Elamcha Urga 86

Keerai Thuvayal 87

Ambe Sasam 88

More Molagai Vathal 89

Vengaya Sambhar 90

Avakkai 91

ARTEKAI PAPPU

Hot and sour lentils with bananas

Ingredients

1 cup split pigeon peas, soaked

2 unripe bananas, cut into 1-inch cubes

2 teaspoons split Bengal gram, roasted

2 teaspoons coriander seeds, roasted

6-8 black peppercorns

2 teaspoons grated coconut

4 dried red chillies

2 tablespoons Tamarind Pulp (page 103)

½ teaspoon turmeric powder

Salt to taste

2 teaspoons oil

½ teaspoon mustard seeds

½ teaspoon cumin seeds

6-8 curry leaves

A pinch of asafoetida

1 tablespoon chopped fresh coriander

Method

1. Pressure cook the pigeon peas and bananas with two cups of water till the pressure is released three times (three whistles).

2. Grind together the roasted Bengal gram, coriander seeds, peppercorns, coconut, red chillies and tamarind pulp to a smooth paste.

3. Mix together boiled pigeon peas, ground paste, turmeric powder and salt in a deep pan.

4. Heat the oil in a separate small pan and add the mustard seeds. When they begin to splutter, add the cumin seeds, curry leaves and asafoetida.

5. Pour the sizzling spices over the *dal* and add the chopped coriander.

6. Bring the mixture to a boil over high heat, stirring continuously. Adjust the consistency and cook for two minutes longer.

7. Serve hot with rice.

Chef's Tip

This *dal* is an intriguing mix of textures and flavours. Include it in your daily repertoire, like I do, because it tastes as wonderful with *roti* as with rice.

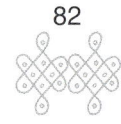

Andhra Pradesh

PARUPPU THUVAYAL

Bengal gram chutney

Ingredients

1 cup split Bengal gram, soaked
8 tablespoons oil
½ teaspoon mustard seeds
6 dried red chillies
2 tablespoons coriander seeds
1 teaspoon cumin seeds
15-20 black peppercorns
1 medium onion, sliced
6 garlic cloves, sliced
½ lemon-sized ball of tamarind
¼ teaspoon asafoetida
Salt to taste

This makes an unusually delicious sandwich spread, or mixed with a little butter, a delightful topping for a canapé. Vary the flavour by using peanuts in place of the dal.

Method

1. Heat the oil in a pan and add the mustard seeds. When they begin to splutter, add the red chillies, coriander seeds, cumin seeds and peppercorns, and sauté for two minutes. Add the onion and garlic and continue sautéing over medium heat for two to three minutes.

2. Drain and add the Bengal gram and tamarind and sauté over high heat for two to three minutes. Mix in the asafoetida and salt.

3. Remove from heat and set aside to cool. Grind to a coarse paste, adding a little water, as required.

4. Serve at room temperature.

Tamil Nadu

INJI-THAKKALI THUVAYAL

Fresh ginger and tomato chutney

Ingredients

1½ inches fresh ginger, roughly chopped
6 medium tomatoes, roughly chopped
10 dried red chillies
3 teaspoons skinless split black gram
6 tablespoons oil
1 teaspoon mustard seeds
¼ teaspoon asafoetida
Salt to taste

Method

1. Wash and pat the red chillies dry and break each one into two. Wipe the split black gram dry.

2. Heat the oil in a pan and add the mustard seeds and asafoetida. When the seeds begin to splutter, add the red chillies and split black gram and sauté till lightly browned.

3. Add the ginger, tomatoes and salt. Stir and cook over low heat till the tomatoes begin to soften. Set aside to cool. Grind the mixture to a slightly coarse texture and serve.

Tamil Nadu

BIRAKAI CHUTNEY

Ingredients

250 grams ridge gourd
10 green chillies, chopped
4 garlic cloves
2 tablespoons chopped fresh coriander
1 tablespoon Tamarind Pulp (page 103)
Salt to taste

Seasoning

1 tablespoon oil
¼ teaspoon mustard seeds
½ teaspoon cumin seeds
3 dried red chillies, broken into large bits
6 curry leaves

Method

1. Scrape the outside of the ridge gourds lightly. Chop roughly.

2. Pound them along with the green chillies, garlic and chopped coriander to a coarse paste. Alternatively, grind them coarsely in a blender.

3. Add the tamarind pulp and salt and mix thoroughly.

4. For the seasoning, heat the oil in a pan; add the mustard seeds, cumin seeds, red chillies and curry leaves. When the mustard seeds begin to splutter, pour the seasoning over the chutney.

5. Serve with rice drizzled with a little ghee.

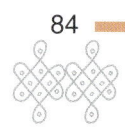

Andhra Pradesh

THAKKALI PACHADI
Tomato chutney

Ingredients
2 small tomatoes, chopped
1 teaspoon oil
¼ teaspoon mustard seeds
¼ teaspoon split black gram skinless
3 dried red chillies, broken
A pinch of asafoetida
1 teaspoon red chilli powder
½ cup yogurt
Salt to taste

Method
1. Heat the oil in a pan and add the mustard seeds, split black grams, red chillies and asafoetida.

2. When the seeds begin to splutter add the tomatoes and red chili powder and sauté for about five minutes over a low heat.

3. Set aside to cool completely. Add the yogurt and salt and mix well. Serve cold.

| *Tamil Nadu* |

VENDAKKAI PACHADI
Ladies' fingers in yogurt

Ingredients
8 ladies' fingers, cut into 1-inch pieces
1 tablespoon oil
¼ teaspoon mustard seeds
1 dried red chilli
¼ teaspoon skinless split black gram
1 tablespoon Tamarind Pulp (page 103)
Salt to taste
1 teaspoon grated jaggery
1 teaspoon rice flour
1 cup yogurt

Method
1. Heat the oil in a deep pan; add the mustard seeds, red chilli and split black gram. When the mustard seeds splutter, add the ladies' fingers and sauté for two-three minutes. Add the tamarind pulp and salt. Cover and cook till done.

2. Add the grated jaggery and mix well. Mix the rice flour with yogurt and add to the *pachadi*. Cook for a minute and remove from heat. Serve at room temperature.

| *Tamil Nadu* |

ELAMCHA URGA

Lemon and date pickle

Ingredients

10 lemons
2 tablespoons vinegar
1½ tablespoons salt
3½ tablespoons sugar
4 garlic cloves
1 inch ginger, chopped
225 grams dates, stoned and roughly chopped
4 tablespoons oil
1 teaspoon cumin seeds
2 teaspoons mustard seeds
2 tablespoons red chilli powder

Method

1. Wash, wipe dry, quarter the lemons and remove all the pips. Place them in a pan along with the vinegar, salt and sugar. Cover the pan and simmer over low heat until the lemons have softened. Remove the lemons and reserve the liquid.

2. Wipe the garlic and ginger dry and grind them along with the dates to a smooth paste.

3. Heat the oil in a pan and sauté the cumin seeds and mustard seeds. Remove from heat and add the reserved liquid used to cook the lemons. Add the chilli powder and return to the heat and stir for a minute.

4. Slowly add the ground date-ginger-garlic paste and one-fourth cup of water and mix well. Finally add the lemons, bring to a boil and cook for a few minutes.

5. Remove from heat and set aside to cool. Pour into a heated sterilised jar and seal while warm.

This pickle is a wonderful accompaniment to Bakala Bhaat (page 72). Some use squeezed-out lemon skins which turns out pretty good too!

Tamil Nadu

KEERAI THUVAYAL

Spinach chutney

Ingredients

1 medium bunch (250 grams) spinach, roughly chopped

1 teaspoon oil

1 tablespoon skinless split black gram

1 tablespoon split Bengal gram

4 dried red chillies

¼ teaspoon asafoetida

1 medium onion, chopped

1 medium tomato, chopped

1 green chilli, chopped

4 tablespoons grated coconut

1 teaspoon Tamarind Pulp (page 103)

Salt to taste

If coriander, mint and roselle can be used for chutney, why not another green leafy vegetable like spinach or 'keerai' in Tamil. An unusual dish which goes well with rice, dosa and idli.

Method

1. Heat the oil in a pan; add the split black gram and split Bengal gram and roast to a golden brown.

2. Add the red chillies, asafoetida, onion, tomato and green chilli; sauté for five minutes.

3. Add the spinach, coconut, tamarind pulp and salt and mix well.

4. Remove from heat and cool. Grind to a fine paste and serve.

Tamil Nadu

AMBE SASAM

Ripe mango-coconut salad

Ingredients

3 medium ripe mangoes
¼ cup green grapes
¾ cup grated coconut
2 dried red chillies (Bedgi), seeded and roasted
¼ teaspoon mustard seeds
1 teaspoon Tamarind Pulp (page 103)
2 tablespoons grated jaggery
Salt to taste

> Contrary to popular belief, this dish is not a dessert but a side dish! It's sweet, it's sour and has the pungency of sasam or mustard seeds.

Method

1. Peel the mangoes, remove the seeds and cut into one-inch cubes.

2. Grind together the coconut, red chillies, mustard seeds and tamarind pulp with one-fourth cup of water into a coarse paste. Add the jaggery and grind once again.

3. Place the mango cubes and grapes in a bowl. Add the salt and the ground spice paste. Mix gently and place in a refrigerator to chill. Serve cold.

Chef's Tip
When mangoes are not in season you can make the *sasam* with other fruit such as ripe bananas, oranges, pineapples and apples.

Karnataka

MORE MOLAGAI VATHAL

Dried buttermilk-flavoured chillies

Ingredients

20 green chillies
½ lemon-sized ball of tamarind
3 teaspoons salt
½ teaspoon coriander seeds
½ teaspoon fenugreek seeds
½ cup buttermilk

> Rice and dal have perfect companions in crisp appalam and vathal of many colours and shapes, including these dried 'curd' chillies.

Method

1. Select chillies which are small and thick. Wash and wipe them dry thoroughly. Slit the chillies.

2. Soak the tamarind in one cup of warm water; strain the pulp. Add one teaspoon of salt and mix well. Soak the prepared chillies in the tamarind mixture overnight.

3. Dry-roast the coriander and fenugreek seeds lightly on a *tawa;* cool and pound to a coarse powder.

4. Mix the remaining salt and the coriander-fenugreek powder with the buttermilk and whisk well.

5. Remove the chillies from the tamarind water and place in the buttermilk. Leave to soak for about three days, or till the chillies turn white.

6. Take the chillies out of the buttermilk and dry in the sun. Reserve the buttermilk. In the evening, put them back into the reserved buttermilk.

7. Repeat this process for two or three days, or till all the buttermilk has been absorbed.

8. Dry the chillies completely in the sun and store in an airtight container.

9. To serve, heat sufficient oil in a *kadai* and deep-fry the chillies in batches, over very low heat, till they turn dark brown and crisp. Drain and serve.

Chef's Tip
These chillies are traditionally served with 'curd-rice' (Bakala Bhaat (page 72) or *thaer sadam*), but go well with any rice dish.

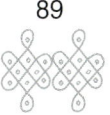

Tamil Nadu

VENGAYA SAMBHAR

Hot and sour lentils with shallots

Ingredients

10 shallots, peeled

¾ cup split pigeon peas

Salt to taste

½ teaspoon turmeric powder

2 tablespoons oil

1 teaspoon mustard seeds

3 dried red chillies, broken into bits

18-20 curry leaves

A generous pinch of asafoetida

1 medium tomato, chopped

4 teaspoons Sambhar Powder (page 103)

1½ tablespoons Tamarind Pulp (page 103)

Method

1. Pressure cook the pigeon peas with salt, turmeric powder and one and a half cups of water till the pressure is released three to four times (three to four whistles). Remove the lid of the cooker when the pressure has reduced completely and mash the *dal* well. Set aside.

2. Heat the oil in a deep pan and add the mustard seeds, red chillies, curry leaves and asafoetida. When the mustard seeds begin to splutter, add the tomato and cook for two to three minutes.

3. Add the shallots and the *sambhar* powder and stir-fry for another four to five minutes.

4. Pour in the *dal* and one cup of water and mix well. Stir in the tamarind pulp and simmer for another five to ten minutes. Serve hot with steamed rice.

> Sambhar comes in many variations… and this one with shallots has the right flavour to dip idli into at a Sunday brunch.

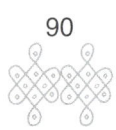

Tamil Nadu

AVAKKAI
Mango pickle

Ingredients

12 medium unripe mangoes

1 cup mustard seeds

2 cups red chilli powder

1½ cups salt

¼ cup turmeric powder

¼ teaspoon asafoetida

4 tablespoons fenugreek seeds

2 cups sesame oil

Method

1. Select good, firm, sour mangoes. Wash thoroughly and wipe them completely dry with a kitchen towel. Cut the mangoes in half with the seed, and then each half into six to eight pieces.

2. Spread them out on a mat and dry in the sun for about two days. Clean and dry the mustard seeds and pound to a coarse powder.

3. Thoroughly mix together the chilli powder, turmeric powder, salt, asafoetida, mustard powder, fenugreek seeds and oil.

4. Remove the seeds from the dried mango pieces and add to the spice mixture.

5. Transfer to a ceramic pickle jar, cover the mouth with a piece of muslin and place in the sun for three days without stirring.

6. Every day from the fourth day onwards, stir the pickle well and continue to place in the sun for at least a week to ten days. This pickle will last for a year.

Chef's Tip
Use only good quality white sesame seed oil and fresh chilli powder.
You may also add chickpeas to this pickle.

Andhra Pradesh

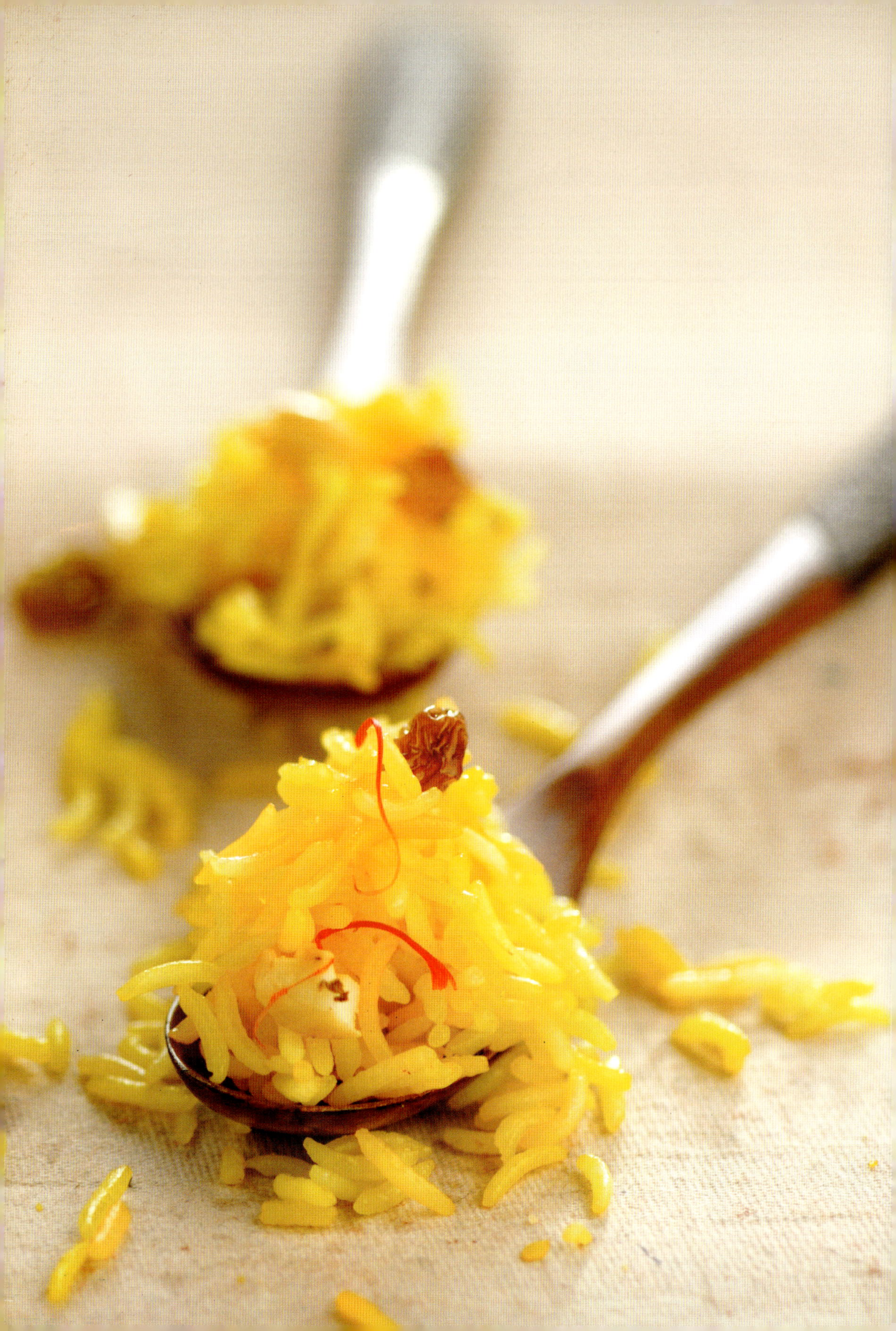

SWEETS

Ada Pradhaman 94

Kesari Bhaat 96

Athirasam 97

Mysore Paak 98

Semiyan Payasam 99

Pal Payasam 100

Sakkarai Pongal 102

ADA PRADHAMAN

Rice pasta in a coconut and jaggery sauce

Ingredients

1 cup *ada* (recipe below)
4 green cardamoms
1 tablespoon sugar
¼ cup pure ghee
12 cashew nuts
2 tablespoons raisins
1½ cups grated coconut
200 grams palm jaggery

Ada

Soak three-fourth cup of rice for about one hour in sufficient water. Drain well. Spread the soaked rice on a piece of cloth to dry for twenty minutes and grind to a fine powder. Sift and mix with one cup of warm water to make a thick paste. Spread the batter on pieces of banana leaf, roll up and fasten with a string. Steam the rolls for fifteen minutes over high heat and cool. Peel the *ada* off the leaves and cut into small dice. Spread out to dry overnight before using. If you wish to store the *ada* for longer, dry well in hot sunlight and store in an airtight container.

Method

1. Grind the cardamoms with the sugar to a fine powder; sift and set aside.

2. Heat two tablespoons of ghee in a pan and fry the ada lightly. Drain and set aside.

3. Heat two more tablespoons of ghee in the same pan and fry the cashew nuts and raisins till light brown.

4. Soak the grated coconut in one cup of warm water, grind and extract thick milk. Repeat the process, make a second extract and set aside. Break the jaggery into smaller pieces.

5. Cook the fried *ada* in one cup of boiling water and the second extract of coconut milk till soft, making sure that they do not get mashed.

6. Add the jaggery and continue cooking till the mixture thickens. Heat the remaining ghee and add to the cooked *ada*.

7. Add the first extract of coconut milk, stir and add the fried cashew nuts and raisins. Stir well and heat through without boiling.

8. Sprinkle the cardamom powder and serve at room temperature.

Kerala

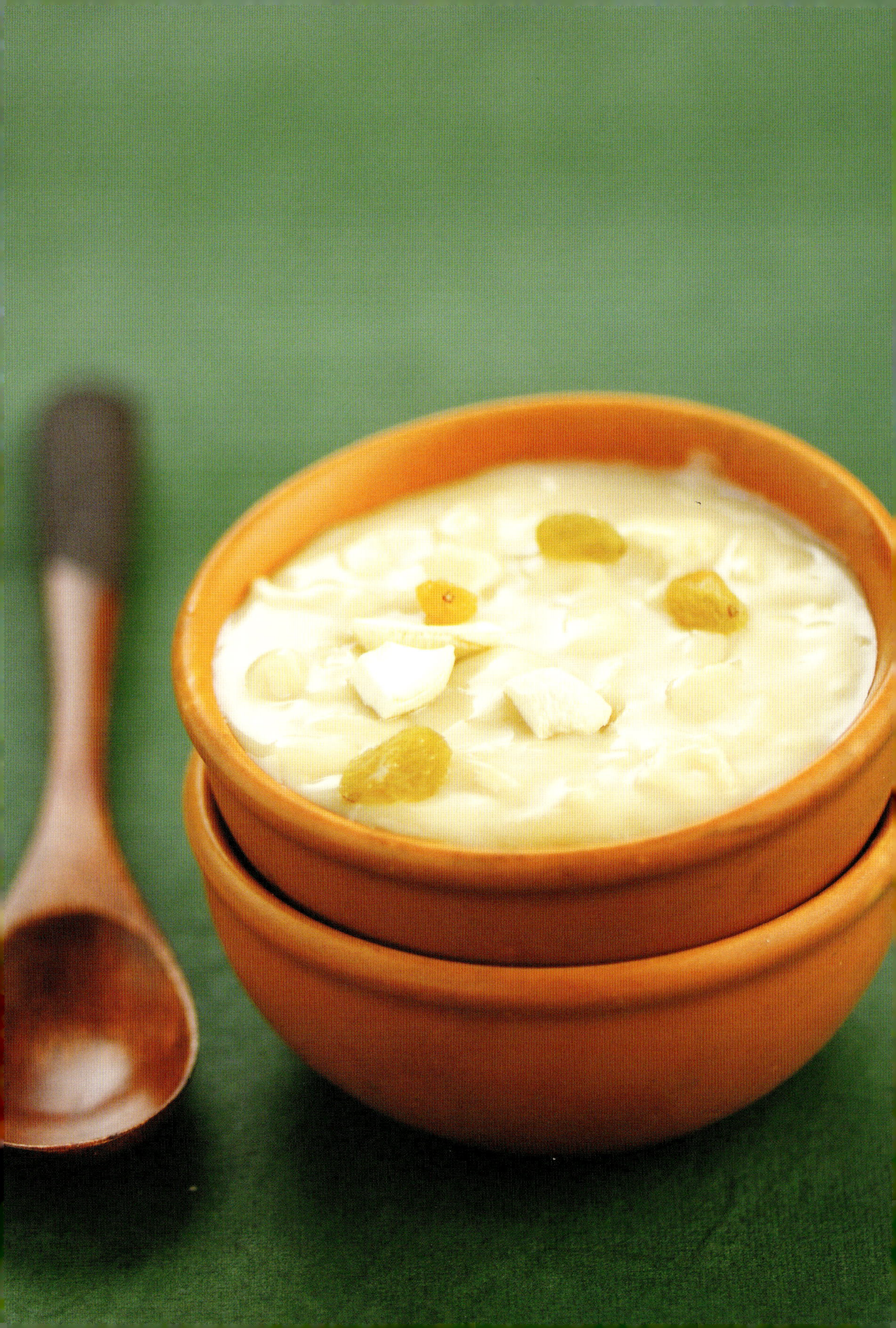

KESARI BHAAT

Saffron-flavoured sweet rice

Ingredients

A few threads of saffron
1 cup Basmati rice, soaked
1 tablespoon pure ghee
2 tablespoons raisins
7-8 cashew nuts, halved
½ cup sugar
½ teaspoon green cardamom powder
25 grams sugar crystals for decoration

All the South Indian states, Goa and Maharashtra too, have a version of this favourite Kannadiga sweet rice dish. Fruits like bananas and pineapple are popular additions to the bhaat.

Method

1. Soak the saffron in one tablespoon of warm water and set aside.

2. Heat the ghee in a pan and sauté the raisins and cashew nuts. Drain and set aside. To the same pan, add the rice and sauté for two to three minutes.

3. Add one and a half cups of boiling water along with the soaked saffron and cook till the rice is partially cooked.

4. Add the sugar and continue to cook till all the water has been absorbed and the rice is soft.

5. Add the cardamom powder and mix gently.

6. Sprinkle the raisins, cashew nuts and sugar crystals and serve hot.

Karnataka

ATHIRASAM

Sweet rice crispies

Ingredients

¾ cup raw rice
½ cup rice flour
1 teaspoon green cardamom powder
¾ cup grated jaggery
Oil for shallow-frying

> A festival delight, it can be stored in an airtight container for a few days.

Method

1. Soak the rice in two cups of water for about two hours. Drain well and spread out on a clean dry piece of cotton in an airy place for twenty minutes. Grind the dried rice to a smooth powder. Add the rice flour and cardamom powder, mix and set aside.

2. Boil the jaggery in half a cup of water. Test the consistency of the syrup by dropping a few drops in a cup of cold water. It should be soft and sticky but should not dissolve in the water. Remove from heat and set aside to cool.

3. Pour the jaggery syrup, a little by little into the rice flour and knead into a soft pliable dough.

4. Divide the dough into twelve equal balls. Flatten each one into a thick round on a greased banana leaf.

5. Heat sufficient oil in a shallow pan and slowly slide the flattened discs into the hot oil.

6. Fry over low heat till both sides turn a dark golden brown and crisp. Remove and drain excess oil by pressing with a spatula. Transfer to absorbent paper to drain completely. Serve hot.

Tamil Nadu

MYSORE PAAK

Gram flour fudge

Ingredients
¾ cup gram flour
4 cups sugar
2½ cups pure ghee

Method

1. Sift the gram flour twice. Heat the ghee in a pan and keep it hot over very low heat.

2. Cook the sugar with two and a half cups of water over medium heat, stirring continuously till it dissolves. Increase the heat and bring the syrup to a boil. Cook without stirring for about five minutes, or till it reaches a single-thread consistency.

3. Add half a cup of hot ghee to the syrup and stir; add the gram flour gradually, stirring all the while to prevent lumps from forming. Stir continuously till the mixture starts bubbling.

4. Pour in the remaining hot ghee, half a cup at a time. Every time you add the ghee, the mixture should sizzle and froth.

5. Continue this process till all the ghee has been used up and there is a pleasant sweet roasted aroma. Pour the mixture into a greased tray. Cool a little and cut into squares.

6. Separate the squares when completely cold and store in an airtight container to retain their freshness and crispness.

> *This sweet has great significance not only at Diwali but also at Tamil weddings. It is usually served to guests with savoury murruku. The bride's luggage will not only contain her personal belongings, but also boxes of Mysore Paak as a going-away gift from her parents.*

Karnataka

SEMIYAN PAYASAM
Vermicelli in sweetened milk

Ingredients
1 cup vermicelli
4 tablespoons pure ghee
8-10 cashew nuts
4 cups milk
1½ cups sugar
A generous pinch of saffron
½ teaspoon green cardamom powder
A pinch of grated nutmeg

Method

1. Heat the pure ghee in a pan; add the vermicelli and sauté for two to three minutes or until light golden brown. Add the cashew nuts, stir well and set aside.

2. Bring the milk to a boil in a thick-bottomed pan. Add the sautéed vermicelli and cashew nuts; mix gently, lower the heat and simmer for five minutes, stirring frequently.

3. Add the sugar and continue to simmer, stirring frequently. Cook for three to four minutes, or until the payasam thickens.

4. Stir in the saffron, cardamom powder and grated nutmeg. Serve hot, at room temperature or chilled.

Milk-based sweets such as this, bind the multi-regional cuisines of India. This payasam is similar to the seviyan kheer of the north.

Tamil Nadu

PAL PAYASAM
Saffron-flavoured rice pudding

Ingredients
1 litre full cream milk
3 tablespoons rice (Kolam)
6-8 saffron threads
2 teaspoons pure ghee
10-12 cashew nuts, chopped
2 teaspoons raisins
½ cup sugar
½ teaspoon green cardamom powder

Method

1. Soak the saffron in one tablespoon of warm milk and set aside.

2. Heat the ghee in a pan and lightly sauté the cashew nuts and raisins and set aside.

3. Bring the remaining milk to the boil in a thick-bottomed pan; add the rice and lower the heat.

4. Cook, stirring continuously, till the rice is cooked and the milk reduces to one-third its original quantity

5. Add the sugar and mix well, crushing the rice lightly while you stir.

6. Add the cardamom powder and saffron-flavoured milk and mix well. Add the sautéed cashew nuts and raisins and mix. Serve hot or cold.

Kheer is considered an auspicious sweet in most regions of the country. In Kerala, this payasam is especially made for Onam.

Kerala

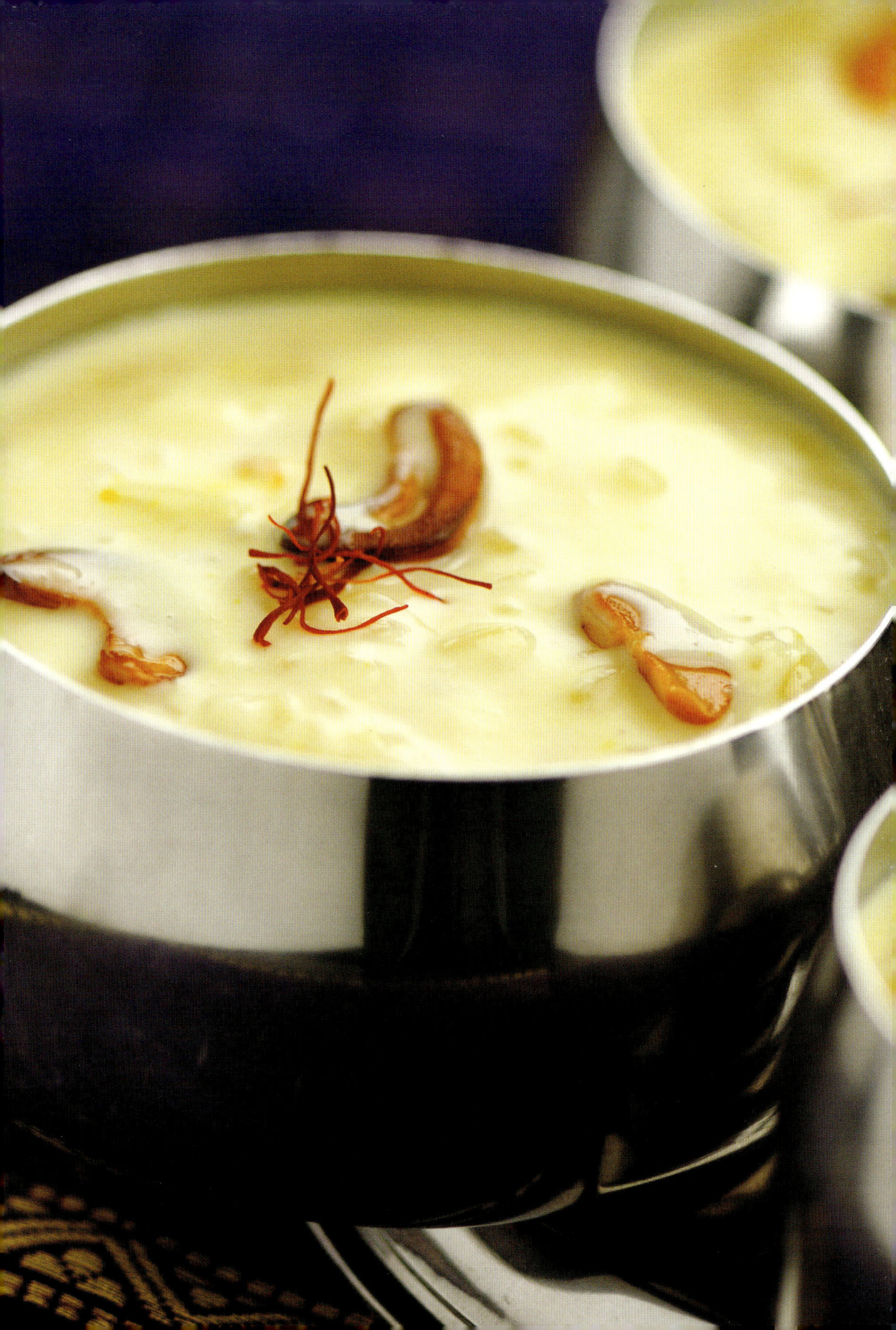

SAKKARAI PONGAL

Sweet rice and lentil pudding

Ingredients

1½ cups rice, soaked

½ cup skinless split green gram

4 green cardamoms

1 tablespoon sugar

2½ cups milk

2 cups grated jaggery

½ cup pure ghee

½ cup grated coconut

¼ teaspoon grated nutmeg

4 tablespoons raisins

12-15 cashew nuts

A pinch of edible camphor powder (optional)

Method

1. Dry-roast the split green gram lightly in a *kadai*. Wash and drain.

2. Grind the cardamoms with the sugar to a fine powder, sift and set aside.

3. Bring the milk with one cup of water to a boil in a thick-bottomed pan.

4. Add the roasted gram and rice to the boiling milk. Bring the mixture to a boil, stirring continuously. Lower the heat, and cook, stirring occasionally, for fifteen minutes or till the rice and gram are completely cooked. You can also pressure-cook the mixture.

5. Add the jaggery and stir continuously to prevent the mixture from sticking to the bottom of the pan. Cook till the jaggery melts completely and is thoroughly incorporated into the rice mixture. Add half the ghee and continue cooking over low heat for about five minutes, stirring frequently.

6. Heat the remaining ghee in a separate pan and fry the coconut lightly. Add the nutmeg, raisins and cashew nuts and stir well. Add this to the cooked *pongal*.

7. Sprinkle the cardamom powder and camphor powder. Stir well and serve hot.

Tamil Nadu

ANNEXURE

COCONUT CHUTNEY

Grind 1 cup grated fresh coconut (white portion only), with very little water into a thick chutney. Add salt. Sauté 2 broken dried red chillies, ¼ tsp mustard seeds and ½ tsp skinless split black gram in 2 tbsp oil. Add a large pinch of asafoetida and 7-8 curry leaves. Pour over the chutney and cover for a while. Mix thoroughly. Variation: add ginger or garlic.

MOLAGA PODI

Dry-roast ½ cup sesame seeds and cool. Heat 2 tbsp sesame oil and sauté ¼ cup skinless split black gram, ¼ cup split Bengal gram and 2 tbsp mustard seeds, separately. Cool. Heat 2 tbsp oil and sauté 3 cups (85 gm) dried red chillies till light brown (do not let blacken). Cool. Grind all roasted ingredients, ¾ tsp asafoetida, 1 tsp grated jaggery and ⅛ cup salt to a coarse powder. Cool and store in a dry airtight bottle. Mix *molaga podi* with liberal quantity of sesame oil or ghee and serve with *idli* or other snacks. Variation: add coconut and tamarind to the *podi*.

RASAM POWDER

Dry-roast 2½ tsp cumin seeds, 1½ tsp coriander seeds, ½ tsp fenugreek seeds, 2 tsp black peppercorns and 5 dried red chillies. Cool. Heat 1 tsp oil in a pan and sauté ⅓ cup split pigeon peas till red. Cool. Grind the roasted ingredients with ½ tsp asafoetida, ½ tsp turmeric powder and 30 curry leaves. Cool and store in an airtight container.

SAMBHAR POWDER

Dry-roast 1 cup coriander seeds, 1 tsp mustard seeds, 1½ tsp cumin seeds, 2 tsp fenugreek seeds and 13 Bedgi dried red chillies. Cool and grind with 20 curry leaves, ¾ tsp asafoetida and ½ tsp turmeric powder. Store in airtight container.

COCONUT MILK

Process 1 cup grated fresh coconut in a blender with ¼ cup warm water. Pass the ground coconut through a piece of muslin or strainer pressing firmly to extract all the juice, or first thick milk. Add a quarter cup of warm water to the strained coconut to get the second, thinner milk from the same solids.

TAMARIND PULP

Soak 75 grams tamarind in 100 ml warm water for 10-15 minutes. Grind to a smooth paste and strain to remove any fibres. Store in an airtight container in the refrigerator.

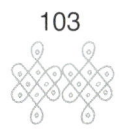

GLOSSARY

ENGLISH	HINDI	ENGLISH	HINDI
Amaranth leaves	Chaulai bhaji	Jaggery	Gur
Asafoetida	Hing	Ladies' fingers	Bhindi
Ash gourd	Safed kumbda	Lemon	Nimbu
Banana, unripe	Kachcha kela	Mace	Javitri
Bay leaves	Tez patta	Mango, ripe	Aam
Beaten rice	Poha	Mango, unripe	Keri
Bengal gram, split	Chana dal	Mint leaves, fresh	Pudina ke taazi pattiyan
Bitter gourd	Karela	Mussels	Teesari
Black gram, skinless, split	Urad dal	Mustard seeds	Rai
Bottle gourd	Lauki	Mutton	Gosht
Brinjals	Baingan	Mutton, minced	Keema
Broad beans	Sem/bakla	Nutmeg	Jaiphal
Buttermilk	Chhach	Peanuts, raw	Kachche moongphali
Camphor, edible	Khane ka kapur	Peas, green	Taaze hare matar
Capsicum, green	Hari Shimla mirch	Peppercorns, black	Kali mirch
Cardamoms, green	Chhoti elaichi	Pigeon peas, split	Toovar dal/arhar dal
Carom seeds	Ajwain	Pomfret	Paplet
Carrot	Gajar	Poppy seeds	Khuskhus
Cashew nuts	Kaju	Potatoes	Aloo
Cauliflower	Phoolgobhi	Potatoes, baby	Chhote aloo
Chicken	Murgh	Prawns	Jheenga
Chicken, boneless	Haddi rahit murgh	Pumpkin	Kumbda
Chillies, dried red	Sookhi lal mirch	Raisins	Kishmish
		Indian salmon	Rawas
Chillies, green	Hari mirch	Refined flour	Maida
Cinnamon	Dalchini	Rice, parboiled	Ukda chawl
Cloves	Laung	Ridge gourd	Turai
Coconut	Nariyal	Roselle leaves	Khatta bhaji
Coriander seeds	Dhania	Saffron	Kesar
Coriander, fresh	Hara dhania	Semolina	Rawa/sooji
Crab	Kekda	Sesame seeds	Til
Cream, fresh	Taazi malai	Shallots	Chhote pyaaz
Cucumber	Kakdi/Kheera	Soda bicarbonate	Khane ka soda
Cumin seeds	Jeera	Spinach leaves	Palak ke taaze patte
Curry leaves	Kadhi patta	Star anise	Chakri phool/badiyan
Dates	Khajoor	Squid	Samudra feni
Drumsticks	Saijan ki phalli	Tamarind	Imli
Fennel seeds	Saunf	Tomatoes	Tamatar
Fenugreek seeds	Methidana	Turmeric powder	Haldi
French beans	Farasi	Vermicelli	Seviyan
Garlic	Lehsun	Vinegar	Sirka
Ginger, fresh	Adrak	Yam	Zamikand/suran
Gram flour	Besan	Yogurt	Dahi
Grapes	Angoor		
Green gram, skinless, split	Moong dal		

104